Contemporary Furniture Plans
114 projects you can build yourself

Ronald P. Ouimet

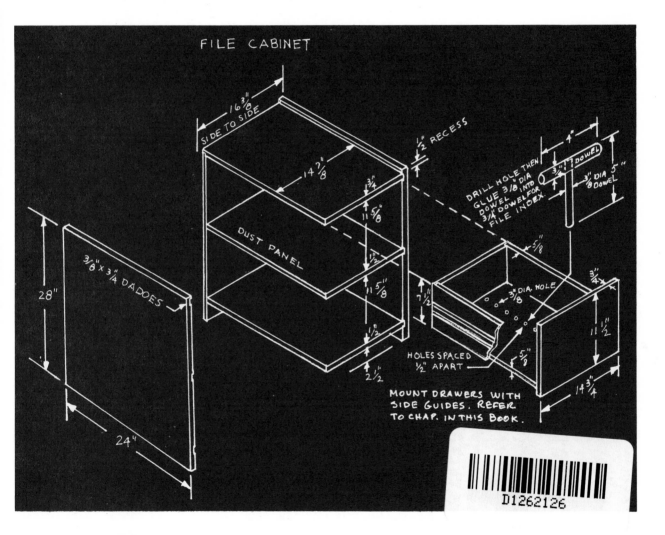

Sterling Publishing Co., Inc.   New York

ACKNOWLEDGMENTS

My sincere thanks to Julie Goddard for her outstanding artistic contribution. I also express my appreciation to Howard and Grace Carley for their past and present support.

Library of Congress Cataloging in Publication Data

Ouimet, Ronald P.
    Contemporary furniture plans.

    Includes index.
    1. Furniture making—Amateurs' manuals. I. Title.
TT185.09   1981   684.1'042   81-8811
ISBN 0-8069-7546-6 (pbk.)   AACR2

Copyright © 1981 by Sterling Publishing Co., Inc.
Two Park Avenue, New York, N.Y. 10016
Distributed in Australia by Oak Tree Press Co., Ltd.
P.O.Box J34, Brickfield Hill, Sydney 2000, N.S.W.
Distributed in the United Kingdom by Blandford Press
Link House, West Street, Poole, Dorset BH15 1LL, England
Distributed in Canada by Oak Tree Press Ltd.
% Canadian Manda Group, 215 Lakeshore Boulevard East
Toronto, Ontario M5A 3W9
Manufactured in the United States of America
All rights reserved

CONTENTS

PREFACE

Modern furniture is very popular, and this popularity increases with each passing year. In its simple unobtrusive forms, contemporary furniture is having a greater influence on modern Americans' taste and modern American interiors. The reasons are obvious: both for utility and aesthetic appeal, modern furniture blends well with the needs of today.

It is the author's desire that this book will serve as a practical guide to fine modern furniture as well as a manual for the home-workshop enthusiast or expert craftsman.

For the amateur or the skilled craftsman, there are working drawings accompanied by illustrations of most of the furniture pieces in a room setting. The preceding text includes a special "how to" section on working processes, including joinery, finishing, gluing, and other important aspects of fine cabinetmaking.

The 114 individual projects shown are for various levels of expertise and equipment. Some are suitable for hand tools, some for portable power tools, and some require woodworking machinery. Many of the pieces are relatively simple to make, others are more difficult undertakings that will satisfy the most advanced cabinetmakers.

This book is dedicated to my family—
Charlotte, Emily, and Elaina

1 equipment and supplies

THE WORKSHOP

In planning a workshop it is necessary to look extensively at your home facilities. The space available may be an entire garage, a room, or such minimal space as a porch. The size of your shop will depend on the type of work you plan for it. If it is to be just a shop for small repairs then the space for tools can be kept down. If the shop is to be used for building and storing furniture pieces then you will need a large-size room such as a garage or basement to handle the necessary footage for machinery and tools. Whatever the size of the shop or wherever it is to be located try to follow a few basic rules: Be sure to have plenty of lighting (natural or artificial), keep the shop well ventilated, allow plenty of working space around major pieces of machinery, store all flammable material in a closed metal container, and keep the shop free of clutter.

Remember, planning a home workshop depends on the facilities, imagination, ingenuity, and safety awareness of the home craftsman.

EQUIPMENT

Hand Tools

First determine how extensively you want to work with wood. Then purchase your equipment. Here is a suggested list of basic hand tools some of which you may have purchased already for general household use.

Rose head countersink bit
Screwdriver bit
Auger bits, ¼–1 inch
Hand drill
Ratchet brace
Twist drills, to ½ inch diameter
Scratch awl
Claw hammer, 14–16 ounce
Wood chisels, ¼–1 inch
Handsaws:
   backsaw, 12-inch
   hacksaw, 12-inch
   coping saw and blades
   ripsaw, 7-point, 26-inch

   crosscut saw, 10–12 point, 26-inch
Planes:
   jack plane, 14-inch
   block plane, 6-inch
Cabinet scraper
Spokeshave
Nailset
Screwdrivers: 8-inch phillips, 8-inch flathead
Combination oilstone
Push-pull measuring tape
2-foot rule
Squares:
   try square
   carpenter's square
Wood files
Wooden mallet
Woodworker's vise
Workbench (refer to plans in book)
Tool panel (can be made from perforated masonite with matching hooks and hangers.

Power Equipment

If the craftsman desires power machinery, his choice will be based upon whether the shop is used simply for home repairs or the building of advanced furniture pieces.

Power table saw, 8- or 9-inch diameter blade
Jig saw, 14-inch throat
Band saw, 14-inch
Drill press, floor or table model
Grinder
Jointer, 4- or 6-inch
Shaper or router
Wood-turning lathe, 36 inches between centers and a 12-inch swing

The craftsman should not use any power machinery without a complete knowledge of its use and capabilities, along with sound safety practices for each machine. Knowledge of machine use and safety precautions should be acquired through adult education courses with a shop instructor or from an experienced craftsman.

LUMBER

HOW LUMBER IS CLASSIFIED

Lumber is either a softwood or a hardwood. Hardwoods come from broad-leafed trees that shed their leaves in the fall. Some examples are oak, mahogany, chestnut, elm, birch, maple, and cherry. Usually hardwoods cost more than softwood; they have a more attractive grain pattern and are used in cabinetmaking and furniture projects.

Softwoods come from needle-bearing, evergreen trees. Typical softwoods are pine, spruce, fir, cedar, and redwood. Softwoods are used in some furniture projects although most softwood is used in house construction due to the moderate cost and easy-working characteristics of softwoods.

HOW LUMBER IS WORKED

If lumber is bought just as it comes from the sawmill the surface of the lumber is rough. It must be surfaced smooth by running it through a machine called a planer before it can be used for building furniture. Lumber usually comes from the lumberyard smoothed (surfaced). It can be bought surfaced on two sides (S2S) or surfaced on four sides (S4S). Due to the lack of an expensive planer in the home workshop, most people purchase lumber already surfaced.

UNDERSTANDING LUMBER SIZES

When purchasing 2 inch × 4 inch (5.1 × 10.2 cm) lumber from a lumberyard you will notice that the actual measurements are $1\frac{5}{8}$ inches × $3\frac{5}{8}$ inches (4.1 cm × 9.2 cm). The original rough board was 2 inches × 4 inches (5.1 cm × 10.2 cm) but became smaller when it was surfaced. The same holds true for all lumber. The actual measured size of a 1-inch (2.5 cm) board is ¾ inch (1.9 cm).

HOW LUMBER IS SEASONED

A newly cut log is green and can contain up to 70 percent moisture. The logs are rough-cut into boards and stacked one on top of the other with spaces in between. They are placed in the open air to dry for one year's time for each inch of board thickness. Lumber dried in this manner is called air-dried lumber (AD). When fully dry the lumber retains approximately 12 to 18 percent moisture content. A better way to season lumber is in a special drying room, similar to a large oven, called a kiln. Kiln-dried lumber (KD) is better for use in furniture projects for it has only 4 to 10 percent moisture content.

GRADING OF HARDWOOD

The finest grade of hardwood is FAS, meaning "first and seconds." This grade is best used in fine furniture construction. Grades number 1 and number 2 have some defects and are lower in quality than FAS.

GRADING OF SOFTWOOD

The select grades of softwoods are grade A and grade B. A and B grades of softwood lumber are used for some furniture projects, also for the trim on the inside of a house. C and D grades of softwood have more knots and defects and are cheaper. Common softwood lumber is only used for rough construction.

ORDERING YOUR LUMBER

In ordering your lumber always specify the following:

The number of pieces

The size of the stock
The kind of wood
The grading of lumber
Surfacing (rough, S2S or S4S)
Seasoning (air-dried or kiln-dried)

PLYWOOD

Plywood is purchased in 4 × 8 foot (1.2 m × 2.4 m) sheets and its thickness is available from ⅛ inch (3.2 mm) to ¾ inch (19.2 mm). For light uses such as the back of a cabinet the ¼-inch (6.4 mm) on up to ½-inch (12.7 mm) thickness will be ample. If a project is to be made with outdoor use in mind, use the exterior grades of plywood. The glue used to bond the layers together is waterproof and it will repel the moisture. The plywood surfaces are graded A, B, C, and D. The A grade represents the smoothest and best grade while the D grade has the most defects and is the least desirable. AA (best grade both sides) is used on projects that will expose both surfaces. Use the less expensive grades for project parts such as shelves, bottoms, backs, and so forth.

Note: when using plywood for furniture projects be sure to always mask exposed edges with matching veneer tape.

TREATMENT OF PLYWOOD EDGES

The end grain of plywood is layered in construction giving it an unattractive appearance. It is best to conceal the end grain and there are a number of ways to achieve this. One way is to miter the corners as a mitered joint will hide the end grain. Another method is to use wood veneer tape (See drawing, this page). The veneer tape can be purchased in most wood grains. The tape is nothing more than a very thin strip of wood approximately ¾ inch (19.2 mm) wide. It is glued to the plywood edges by applying it evenly with pressure from the hand. Be sure to align it correctly.

Another method of concealing the plywood edge is by using matching molding, which will provide a decorative edge. Molding can also be purchased in metal or plastic; either is excellent for an edge that receives a lot of use.

WOOD VENEER TAPE

METAL OR PLASTIC EDGE

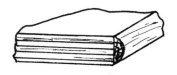

HALF ROUND WOOD MOLDING

WOOD MOLDING

HARDBOARD

Standard hardboard can be purchased in 4-by-8-foot (1.2 m × 2.4 m) sheets and is available in ⅛-inch (3.2 mm) to ¼-inch (6.4 mm) thickness. Hardboard is excellent for use in general cabinetwork such as drawer bottoms and cabinet backs and can be purchased with holes spaced approximately 1 inch (2.5 cm) apart. Perforated hardboard accompanied with the proper hooks is excellent for storing tools and equipment and lends itself well for the backs of stereo cabinets. If the project containing the hardboard is to be outdoors or in any way exposed to moisture, use tempered hardboard.

Other members of the hardboard family are chipboard, flake board, and particle board. These hardboards can be purchased in a ¾-inch (19.2 mm) thickness and have a much coarser grain. One disadvantage of working with hardboard is its lack of holding power with fasteners. Screws and nails will stand up to more pressure in solid wood and plywood than they do in hardboard.

HARDWARE

SCREWS

When purchasing screws specify the length and diameter. Numbers 1 to 16 indicate the diameter. If the screw shank is a #16 it is the largest diameter, if it is #1 it is the smallest. See the drawings on this page of the most common woodworking screws. When drilling into plywood or hardwood always use a pilot hole. Use a shank or clearance hole in the first piece of wood when screwing two pieces of stock together. The shank or clearance hole allows the two pieces to fit together tightly. Without the shank hole the first piece tends to "stay out" from the second piece, preventing a tight fit. For proper appearance it is always wise to set a flathead screw into a countersink or a counterbored hole. If a counterbored hole is used fill it with a furniture button or dowel plug. (See drawing below.)

FLATHEAD   ROUNDHEAD   OVALHEAD

FOR USE IN GENERAL FASTENING OF WOODWORKING JOINTS

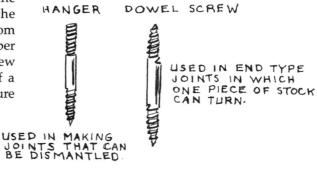

HANGER   DOWEL SCREW

USED IN MAKING JOINTS THAT CAN BE DISMANTLED.

USED IN END TYPE JOINTS IN WHICH ONE PIECE OF STOCK CAN TURN.

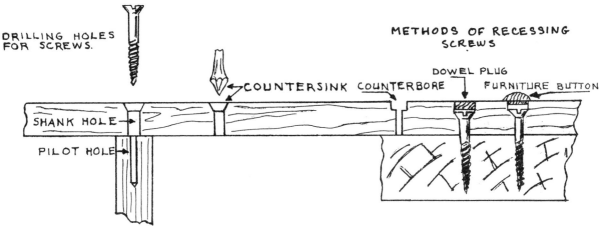

DRILLING HOLES FOR SCREWS.

METHODS OF RECESSING SCREWS

COUNTERSINK   COUNTERBORE

DOWEL PLUG

FURNITURE BUTTON

SHANK HOLE→

PILOT HOLE→

NAILS

When purchasing nails refer to the size as "penny" (abbreviated D or d). The drawing of a box nail is made into a simple chart to show the penny size in comparison to inches.

Common nails have heavy, flat heads and are used for general purpose work. Box nails are relatively thin and have flat heads. They were first used for nailing together boxes built of wood that was thin and easy to split. Finish and casing nails have small heads that can be set beneath the wood surface. They are used for furniture, cabinet, and trim work. Brads are small finishing nails and are used to nail thin stock such as molding.

Use a nailset to drive a casing, finish, or brad nail beneath the surface of the wood.

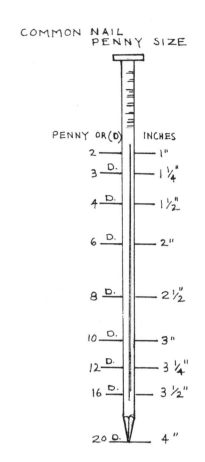

COMMON NAIL
PENNY SIZE

PENNY OR (D)	INCHES
2	1"
3 D.	1¼"
4 D.	1½"
6 D.	2"
8 D.	2½"
10 D.	3"
12 D.	3¼"
16 D.	3½"
20 D.	4"

NAILSET

NAIL SET AND FILLED

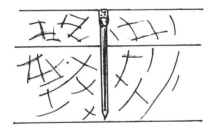

BRACES AND FASTENERS

Metal braces are supports used in making 90° angled joints. The "inside corner brace" is a strip of metal with screw holes drilled through it; it is bent to a 90° angle to form an L-shape, which is excellent for bracing corners. The T-plate is nothing more than a flat drilled plate made in the shape of a T. It screws flat onto the surface of the work. The flat corner plate is used for the same support purposes except that it is shaped like an L. A mending plate has a drilled straight shape and is used for support in straight lines.

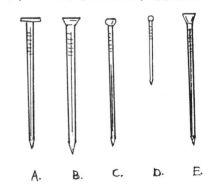

TYPES OF NAILS (A) BOX (B) COMMON
(C) FINISH (D) BRAD (E) CASING

A. B. C. D. E.

CORNER BRACE

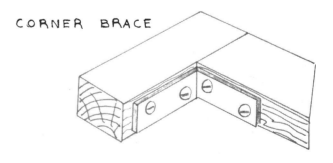

These braces are ideal for use in repair work and construction of light framed cabinets, etc. Be sure and use the braces only where they will be concealed or where appearance does not matter.

If maximum strength is not required in a joint, a corrugated metal fastener can be used. Corrugated fasteners are best suited for light work such as screen and picture frames and simple box construction. Corrugated fasteners are sharpened on one edge for ease in driving them into the joint. Before installing the fastener into the joint be sure that the joint is held together as tightly as possible.

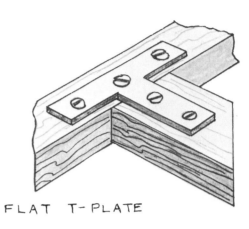

FLAT T-PLATE

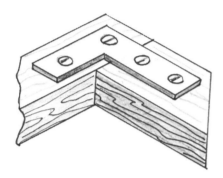

FLAT CORNER PLATE

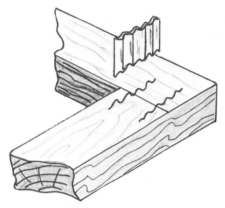

CORRUGATED FASTENER

FURNITURE GLIDES AND CASTERS

When determining if your furniture project needs a glide or a caster just ask yourself this simple question: Do I plan to move the furniture piece often or leave it stationary? If you don't plan to move it frequently, use a glide; otherwise, a caster is best.

You can purchase glides in a variety of sizes and with the choice of steel or plastic material for the bottom. The nail-type glide is the easiest to install although it is not adjustable. The screw-type glide must have a hole drilled for the diameter of the screw, and it can be adjusted to various heights for an uneven floor or an uneven project base.

Casters are available in two styles, the adjustable stem caster and the nonadjustable plate caster. The stem caster must have a hole drilled into the base of the furniture piece. The drilled hole is made to accept the sleeve which in turn receives the stem of the caster.

The plate caster is simply screwed to the base bottom. This type of caster cannot be adjusted to various heights.

In order to facilitate swiveling, all casters are constructed with ball bearings. Casters can be purchased with either plastic or rubber wheels. The rubber wheel type is best suited to a hard surface such as slate, wood, or concrete. The

CASTERS

PLATE CASTER

ADJUSTABLE STEM CASTER.

plastic wheel type of caster is best used on soft surfaces such as carpet.

To stop the furniture piece from rolling, use the locking type of caster. The caster locks in place by means of a small lever on the outside of the wheel.

FURNITURE GLIDES

NAIL GLIDE

ADJUSTABLE SCREW GLIDE

NAIL GLIDE

CLAMPS

The clamps used most often in cabinet and furniture making are the bar, hand-screw, and C-clamp. Each of these clamps has a particular use and each clamp works by the hand-screw adjustment. When clamping, it is wise to have plenty of clamps on hand for the job being done. Arrange the clamps in advance so that they clamp onto the project with a minimum of adjustment.

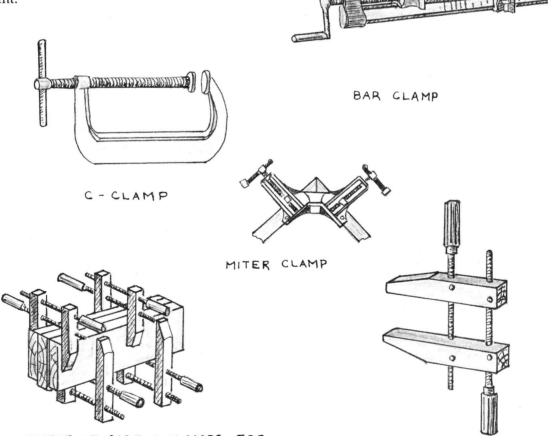

BAR CLAMP

C - CLAMP

MITER CLAMP

ARRANGEMENT OF SCREW CLAMPS FOR CLAMPING BOARDS TO INCREASE THICKNESS.

HAND SCREW CLAMP

THREE COMMON HINGES USED IN MODERN FURNITURE

BUTT HINGE

MUST BE GAINED INTO THE DOOR AND FRAME. THEY PRESENT AN UNOBTRUSIVE APPEARANCE AND COME IN A VARIETY OF SIZES.

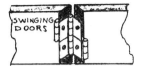

DOUBLE-ACTING HINGES

ALLOW A DOOR TO BE SWUNG FROM BOTH DIRECTIONS

PIVOT HINGE

COMES IN A VARIETY OF SHAPES AND PRESENT AN UNOBTRUSIVE APPEARANCE.

GLUES

Today the variety of glues available to the consumer seems to be almost endless. Therefore I will deal only with the most commonly used glues on the market.

Polyvinyl Acetate (PVA)

This is an excellent glue for most household projects such as ceramic work, craft work, and furniture construction. PVA glue will give an excellent bond but cannot withstand excessive moisture or high temperatures. This glue should set for at least 8 hours in a 65° to 70°F temperature.

Polyvinyl Chloride (PVC)

This is an excellent waterproof adhesive used on wood, metal, china, glass, or porcelain. The drying time varies, therefore brand specifications should be followed.

Cellulose Glue

This is best suited for small repairs to furniture, model work, is superior for joining chinaware and glass, and can be used on most fabrics.

It gives a fast-drying, colorless joint. The bond strength is increased by applying two coats to both surfaces.

Epoxy Glue

This glue is excellent for joining glass and metals, as well as for china repairs. These adhesives are waterproof and oil resistant. They are excellent for bonding dissimilar materials, such as plastic to metal, glass to metal or glass to concrete, etc. Epoxy glues are made in regular and fast-setting types. They are two-part glues—a resin and a hardener that are mixed in equal amounts.

Liquid Hide Glue

This is the traditional glue used by cabinetmakers. It is best suited for furniture repair and construction. Hide glue makes an excellent bond that holds up well under a heavy load. Do not use hide glue on projects that will be exposed to water or high humidity.

2 construction guides

JOINTS

Woodworking joints are of two categories: "lay-up" and "assembly." Lay-up joints are used for building up the dimension of stock. Assembly joints are those used in assembling members which have been cut to a certain shape and dimension.

A joint's characteristics are to provide strength and appearance. Most joints are held together by the use of such fasteners as nails, screws, corrugated fasteners, wedges, or pins. Glue is used as an adhesive when a metal or wood fastener is not desired. The strength of a woodworking joint depends largely on an accurate fit and the quality of workmanship in applying the fasteners or adhesive. When clamping with several bar clamps it is advised that the clamps be placed alternately one up and the next one down, thus preventing the surface from buckling. Clamps should be placed approximately 18 inches (.5 m) to 24 inches (.6 m) apart.

LAY-UP OR EDGE JOINTS

Butt Joints

The butt joint is the most common joint. It is constructed by butting together one member (end or edge) to the end, edge, or surface of another. It is secured by using glue, nails, or screws. It is the weakest joint to use and should not be used where it will receive a lot of pressure. The dowel, spline, or half-lap joints are recommended.

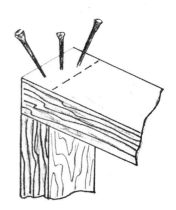

NAILED JOINT
TWO-THIRDS OF THE NAIL
LENGTH SHOULD BE IN
THE SECOND PIECE.

TOE NAILING
NAILS ARE DRIVEN IN FROM OPPOSITE
SIDES AT APP. 30° TO 40° ANGLE.

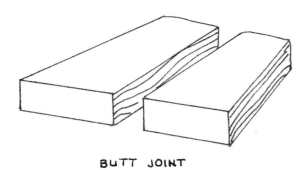

BUTT JOINT

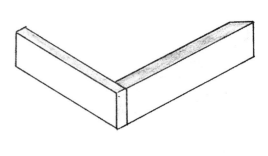

END BUTT JOINT

Tongue-and-Groove Joints

The tongue-and groove joint is made by cutting two rabbets of equal dimensions on one board's edge to achieve the tongue, then by continuing to cut a groove to the width and depth of the tongue on the matching board. Fasten together with glue and clamps. The tongue-and-groove opening should not exceed half the thickness of the stock.

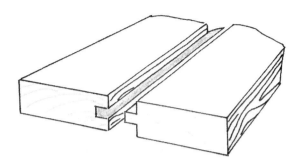

TONGUE-AND-GROOVE JOINT

ASSEMBLY JOINTS

Butt Joints

The simple butt joint is the weakest method used in assembling cut parts. The butt joint is constructed by butting one piece of wood to another at a right angle. The surface contact made is with the end grain. The end grain is extremely porous which makes it difficult to glue. The butt joint should be reinforced with glue blocks screwed to the inside for added strength.

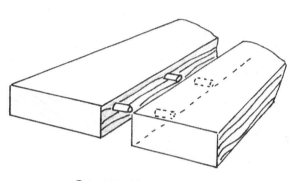

DOWEL JOINT

Doweled Joints

The doweled joint is used to give added strength to the butt joint by adding resistance to the cross-strain of the stock. Drill holes for the dowel pins in the edges of the two pieces to be joined. Use a doweling jig for accuracy. Apply glue to dowel pins and board edges. Insert the dowels in one piece and continue to line up the piece. Join them together using clamps.

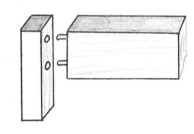

DOWELED END JOINT

SPLINE JOINT

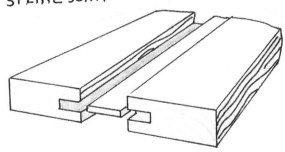

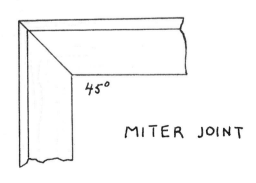

45°

MITER JOINT

Miter Joints

A miter joint is a butt joint in which two pieces of stock are cut at the same angle, usually 45°, in order to form a 90° angle. Because the joined surfaces are end grains the joint is weak and should be reinforced with a spline, dowels, or corrugated fasteners.

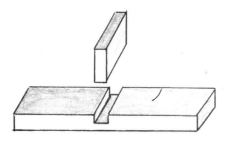

DADO JOINT

Dado Joints

A dado joint is often confused with a groove joint. A dado is a recess cut across the grain of wood, into which another board is fit. A groove is a recess cut with the grain of wood.

The dado-and-groove joints should never exceed more than one-half to two-thirds the thickness of the stock in which they are being cut. The joint should fit snugly and the depth of the cut must be even.

Half-Lap Joints

This joint has remarkable strength and is one of the most often used right-angled joints. It is constructed by cutting away half the thickness of each member to be joined so that when fastened together a thickness equal to that of one member is formed.

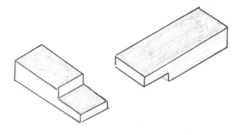

**END LAP JOINT
HALF LAP**

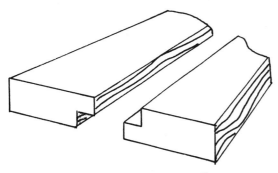

RABBET JOINT OR HALF LAP

Rabbet Joints

A rabbet joint is a recess cut along the end or edge of a board. It is usually used in panel and drawer construction. The cut recess should be one-half to two-thirds the thickness of the stock. The rabbet joint should form a 90° angle.

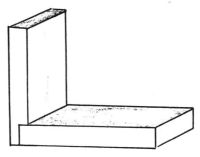

RABBET JOINT

JOINT PREPARATION

Joint preparation is extremely important because even the thinnest film of dust, dirt, or oil will prevent an adhesive from bonding correctly. To bond wood joints, be certain that the surfaces are square and sanded properly; all sanding dust must be cleaned off the surfaces before applying the glue.

It is important that the joints are fitted tightly with the use of clamps such as bar clamps, screw clamps, and spring clamps. Repairs made to china, glass, and plastic are clamped with such makeshift devices as small jigs, masking tape, or elastic bands.

If a wood joint is loose it can be tightened up by filling the space with a small wood sliver. Cut the sliver to the size needed then apply glue to it. Press the sliver into the gap. For smaller jobs use a crack-filling adhesive such as plastic wood.

GLUING AND CLAMPING YOUR STOCK

1. Make adjustments to the clamps to fit your gluing job.
2. Cut protective blocks for the bar clamps. Prepare pieces of wood for alignment across the ends.
3. Start with a trial assembly; do not use glue on the pieces. This is to check for correct fit of all joints and surfaces. Now, disassemble the pieces to apply the glue.
4. Set up V-cut jigs or a clamp donkey to hold the bar clamps in position.
5. Rapidly spread the glue evenly on all jointed surfaces that will come in contact with each other.
6. Assemble the boards together by fastening the clamps as shown in the drawing. Place the bar clamps approximately 15 inches (38.1 cm) apart. It is wise to use wood blocks to protect the edges of the wood from the metal clamp. It is also helpful to have a friend help you in this type of clamping operation. If the boards buckle, align them with boards positioned on the top and bottom of the ends held in place with C-clamps or hand-screw clamps. Use paper between the end boards and the project being glued; this will prevent the boards from sticking to the surface. When gluing up stock to obtain additional thickness use plenty of hand-screw clamps.
7. To remove excess glue before it hardens use a damp sponge or a scraper. All glue should be removed from the surface before any finish is applied. *Note*: Glue is a nonporous material that will not allow stain or finish to penetrate through; therefore, it will leave an unsightly glue line on your project's surface if not cleaned up.

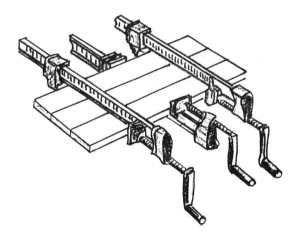

ARRANGEMENT OF CLAMPS
FOR EDGE GLUING.

FURNITURE CONSTRUCTION

BOX CONSTRUCTION

Box construction is the easiest of all cabinet and furniture fabrication. It is used for the construction of drawers, chests, and numerous types of boxes. It consists of a simple four-sided box with a bottom and often a top lid. The boards used in box construction always have the grain running in the same direction on all four sides. The corners are joined with butt, rabbet, or more difficult joints. The bottom is usually inset into a groove or rabbet cut.

CASE CONSTRUCTION

Units such as kitchen cabinets, stereo cabinets, and bookcases are examples of case construction. Case construction is simply a box turned on its side; therefore, the methods of construction are similar to box-construction techniques. The corners are joined with a miter, rabbet, or similar joint. A rabbet is cut around the rear edges so that the back will fit into it. The back would most likely be plywood or hardboard. In case construction, the same material serves as both interior and exterior of the assembled structure. If the structure has fixed shelves they are usually installed into dado joints although they can be held in place by means of nail and screw fasteners. If movable shelves are desired they are usually mounted on adjustable shelf brackets which can be purchased in various lengths and styles. The adjustable track can be installed flat to a surface or it can be recessed into a groove cut to its size. Plywood and other types of sheet material work well in case construction. If plywood is used for construction, however, it is advisable to face or nose the exposed front edge.

FRAME CONSTRUCTION

Frame and case construction appear to be similar although the fabrication techniques differ. In frame construction the material used to cover the frame is usually of lighter weight. Instead of using ¾-inch- (19.2 mm) thick solid wood for the cover it would be ½-inch- (12.7 mm) thick plywood or particle board. Prefabricated bathroom vanities and kitchen cabinets are usually constructed this way. The cabinet frames are most likely to be ¾ inch (19.2 mm) thick by 1½ inches (3.8 cm) to 2 inches (5.1 cm) wide. The front stiles (vertical members) of the frame usually overlap the sides to conceal the cheaper edges of the frame cover material.

LEG-AND-RAIL CONSTRUCTION

Leg-and-rail construction is comprised of four rails and four legs, usually confined to furniture construction. The common methods of joining the corners are the mortise-and-tenon and dowel joint, reinforced by corner glue blocks or various metal hardwares. Of the two corner joints the various dowel joints are easier to construct. The difficulties are in keeping the holes completely aligned in the construction of a dowel joint and to use a good adhesive for maximum strength.

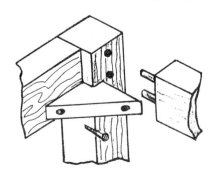

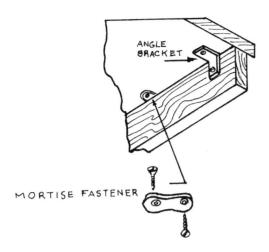

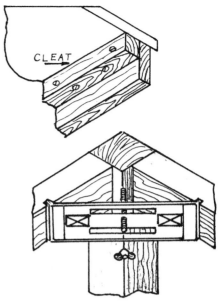

When securing a top to the leg-and-rail assembly one may use cleats or special metal hardware.

HOW TO CONSTRUCT FRAME PANELS

Most frame panels are used in doors placed in cabinet and furniture construction. The frame surrounding the panel consists of two vertical side members called stiles and two horizontal top and bottom members called rails.

The stiles and rails are always constructed of solid wood and they range from ¾ inch (19.2 mm) to 1 inch (2.5 cm) thickness to 1½ inches (3.8 cm) to 2½ inches (6.5 cm) in width. There are numerous methods for securing the corners of the stiles and rails ranging from mortise-and-tenon joint, dowel joint, lap joint, butt joint, and miter joint. The panel is fastened into a groove cut in the frame. The panel can also be placed in a rabbet instead of a groove. The rabbet cut is always used for placement of glass, mirrors, or Plexiglas. The panel can be solid stock or standard sheet stock such as hardboard or plywood. Some fine pieces of furniture often have raised panels or various decorative cutouts and carvings in the panels and rails.

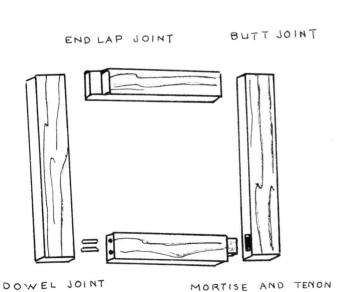

PLAIN PANEL FRAME WITH
STENCIL

RAISED PANEL FRAME

CONSTRUCTING A RAISED PANEL

In making a raised panel it is necessary to use only solid wood stock glued up to the correct width. Adjust the tilting arbor of a table saw to approximately a 10° to 12° angle, with the depth of cut ranging from 1 inch (2.5 cm) to 3½ inches (8.9 cm). The table saw rip fence should be placed approximately ³⁄₁₆ inch (4.8 mm) to ¼ inch (6.4 mm) away from the highest point of the tilted blade. Proceed to make a cut on all four edges, using the 10° to 12° angled setting.

Return the tilted blade back to a 90° angle and adjust the depth of cut to approximately ⅛ inch (3.2 mm). Set the rip fence so that the saw cut will intersect the first angled cut at its full depth. Proceed to cut all four edges in completing the camfered cut. Set the panel into a precut groove or rabbet in the frame. *Note*: If a plain or raised panel is set into a frame with a rabbet cut, it should be held in place by the use of ¾-inch (19.2 mm) half-round molding, lapped over both frame and panel.

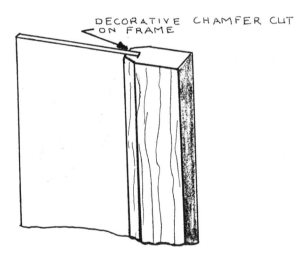

DECORATIVE CHAMFER CUT
ON FRAME

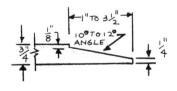

CHAMFER CUT FOR
RAISED PANEL

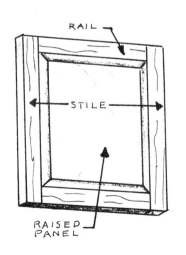

24

HOW TO CONSTRUCT DRAWERS

There are two basic drawers most likely used in furniture and cabinet construction, the flush-front drawer and the lip-front drawer. The difference between the two is that the lip-front drawer has an overlap of ⅜ inch (9.6 mm) on all sides, while the flush drawer fits flush into the front of a cabinet frame. The lip-front drawer fits into the cabinet frame although the ⅜ inch overlap partially covers the cabinet frame.

Simple box construction is used for the fabrication of drawers, the box-construction techniques mentioned previously in this chapter. Simply put, drawers consist of two sides, a front, a back, and bottom. Corner joints can consist of the simple butt joint requiring simple tools, but quality drawers may have the difficult dovetail joint requiring more time and electric power tools. The medium-difficult corner joint is the rabbet joint. The bottom is usually ¼-inch (6.4 mm) to ⅜-inch (9.6 mm) plywood, and it is fitted into a groove placed approximately ½ inch (12.7 mm) above the bottom edge of the two sides and back. You should practice care in fastening a drawer together. It should be assembled with glue and nails except for the bottom which is left free in its groove because of swelling and shrinking of the drawer. It is very important to construct the drawer 90° square, for a drawer out of square is extremely difficult to fit into the cabinet opening.

FLUSH DRAWER

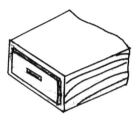

LIPPED DRAWER

Assemble a drawer after the furniture or cabinet in which it fits has been constructed, so that you can fit the drawer to the cabinet opening. Start by determining the type of drawer front, flush front, or lip front for the cabinet. Be careful in trying to match the grain and color of the wood for a more than one-drawer cabinet.

The front of the drawer is usually ¾ inch (19.2 mm) thick, while the sides and back are ½ inch (12.7 mm) thick. Try to select stock that is not warped and is free of knots. Pine and oak are good woods for the sides and back. A ⅜-inch (9.6

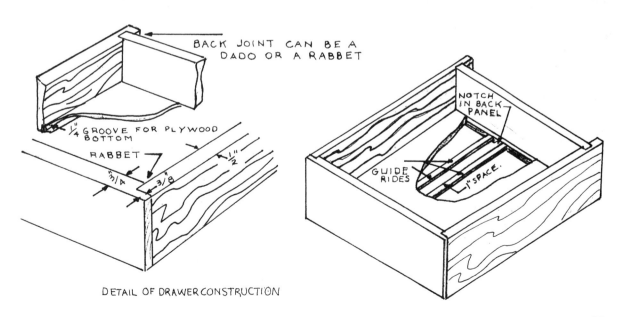

DETAIL OF DRAWER CONSTRUCTION

mm) overlap drawer is safest to use for it will cover the drawer opening even if it shrinks. The 3/8-inch-lip (9.6 mm) drawer front should be 3/4 inch (19.2 mm) longer and 3/4 inch (19.2 mm) wider than the cabinet opening. A flush drawer front should be 1/8 inch (3.2 mm) less than the length of the cabinet drawer opening and 1/16 inch (1.6 mm) less in width of the opening.

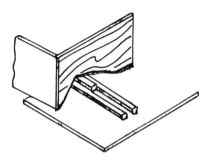

CENTER GUIDE

HOW TO CONSTRUCT DRAWER GUIDES

Most of the projects in this book require drawer guides. There are several styles of wooden guides although the choice should be based on the size of drawer that they are used with. Small drawers do not need guides or they may just need a simple strip glued to each side while larger drawers, which carry more weight, require stronger guides.

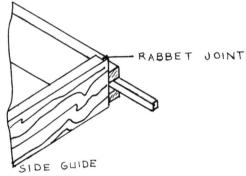

RABBET JOINT

SIDE GUIDE

A GROOVE CAN BE CUT INTO THE DRAWER SIDE IN PLACE OF THE TWO STRIPS.

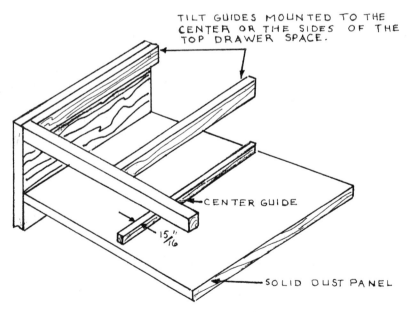

TILT GUIDES MOUNTED TO THE CENTER OR THE SIDES OF THE TOP DRAWER SPACE.

CENTER GUIDE

15/16"

SOLID DUST PANEL

The single center guide is nothing more than a simple 1/2-inch-by-1-inch (12.7-mm by 2.5-cm) piece of stock fastened in the center of a dust panel or drawer divider board located under the drawer bottom. Glued on the drawer bottom are two 1/2-inch-by-1-inch (12.7-mm by 2.5-cm) guide rides which override the center guide placed on the dust panel. It is necessary to cut a notch in the back-drawer panel to match the opening created by the two guide rides. The most simple method of making a single center guide is by just using a 1/2-inch-by-1-inch notch cut in the center-back-drawer panel to track on the center guide. A top guide is used to prevent the drawer from tilting down when the drawer is opened.

Side guides are fastened to the lower corners of larger drawer openings. In using this guide technique, it is necessary to use a top guide to prevent the drawer from tilting down when opened.

If a drawer is to be placed directly under a table top the drawer side guides are constructed in the shape of an L. The L-shaped guides are secured under the table top and guide rider strips are fastened flush to the top edge of the drawer sides.

NOTE: It may be necessary to use soap or wax occasionally on the guides and riders to assure a smooth opening and closing of the drawer.

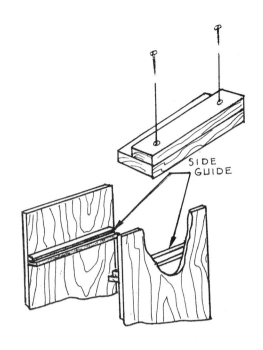

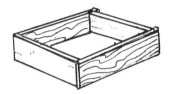

Commercial Drawer Guides

There are a multitude of commercial drawer guides available. Perhaps the best guide is the roller type coupled with bearings, for it will withstand the heavy load commonly found in dressers, file drawers, and kitchen cabinet drawers.

NOTE: If the drawer is mounted with metal or wood side guides, the space between the side of the drawer and the side of the cabinet should be at least ½ inch (12.7mm). (Check manufacturers' instructions for exact clearance on metal guides.)

HOW TO CONSTRUCT DOORS

Like drawers, most doors assembled to furniture are of flush or lip construction. The material used for doors can be of plywood, solid stock, or frame and panel. Lip doors are made to set over the frame of the cabinet exactly in the same way drawer fronts overlap. The door is always cut ¾ inch (19.2 mm) longer and wider than the cabinet opening to allow for the ⅜-inch (9.6 mm) lip. On the inner edge of the door is a ⅜-inch-wide and ⅜-inch-deep cut made completely around to allow the door to fit over the frame. The door is

hung to the frame with a semi-concealed ⅜-inch (9.6 mm) offset hinge.

A flush door is fitted to the cabinet opening in the same manner the flush-front drawer is fitted to its opening. The door should be approximately ¹⁄₁₆ inch (1.6 mm) narrower and ⅛ inch (3.2 mm) less in width than the cabinet door opening. When installing a flush door either butt or surface hinges are used.

Sliding doors are easier to install than swinging doors. Generally they are made of lighter stock than conventional doors. You can purchase track for sliding doors made from plastic or aluminum, or the track can be made by cutting matching grooves into the top and bottom of the framework.

Grooves must be cut before the cabinet is assembled. It is important to cut the upper grooves approximately twice as deep as the bottom grooves so that the doors can be lifted up, then lowered into place.

Use silicone spray or wax in the grooves for easy sliding of the doors. If handles are to be used make them thin enough so there will be no interference when the doors bypass each other.

NOTE: Handles can be recessed into the doors.

FINISHING THE PROJECT

It is crucial that the project be carefully sanded to a smooth surface before any application of finish. Although power sanders may help to do much of the sanding only careful hand sanding can bring a professional result. It is foolish to think that stain or paint will conceal a poorly prepared surface. On the contrary, they tend to show up a poorly prepared surface.

Sanding of the project should be done in stages starting with 60- to 80-grit paper for rough work, continued with 120- to 150-grit paper for smoothing the project. To produce a smoother surface work with 220- to 280-grit paper. It is good practice to do all sanding in a straight line with the grain of the wood.

Splits, checks, or nail holes should be filled with plastic wood or stick shellac. These products can be purchased in a multitude of colors to match the color of your wood or stain.

A finish should not be applied under extreme conditions of dampness or cold.

The purpose of staining is twofold: It is translucent which allows it to emphasize the beauty of the grain, and it allows you to bring your project to your desired color.

When staining your project, place it in an area that will receive the same amount of light that the project will receive when in use.

STAINING YOUR PRODUCT

There are several types of stains, oil and dye stains being the two most common. They are applied in a liquid state and given varying amounts of drying time. When the stain has been thoroughly dried the surface should be given several coats of clear varnish, linseed oil, or lacquer for protection.

Oil Stains

These are composed of finely ground powders mixed to a paste with benzine or turpentine. These stains can be applied with a rag or brush. The stain can be rubbed on in any direction and should be given 15 to 20 minutes to dry. At this time it should be rubbed off in the direction of the grain with a clean cloth. If the color tone is too light allow the first coat to dry overnight and then apply a second coat.

Dye Stains

These stains normally are water and alcohol based. They soak into the wood very fast, therefore, should be applied in very light coats. Dye stains are known for their quality in rich colors and their ability to bring out the grain characteristics of wood. These stains must be mixed for they come in a powdered form. They can be applied by spraying, brushing, sponging, or using a rag. Mixing the powder is done with hot water. The advantages of mixing your own stain are that if your color is too light it can be darkened by adding more powder; dark colors can be made lighter by adding more water. Two coats of stain should be applied to bring it to its best results.

One disadvantage of a water-base stain is that it raises the grain of the wood. Allow it to dry overnight, then sand the surface lightly with 280 grit sandpaper to remedy this problem.

Alcohol-base stains have the advantage of not raising the grain of wood and also of being sold premixed in a variety of colors. Their color intensity can be reduced by adding alcohol to the stain.

They can be applied to the wood by wiping with a rag, spraying, or by using a brush.

Safety precautions you should follow are: 1) Wear gloves when applying; 2) Do not work near open flame or high temperature; 3) Do not smoke while applying the stain.

Varnish

There are many grades and colors of varnish available and they are bought ready to use. The better grades will expand and contract with the wood they are applied to without cracking. The colors are clear to dark brown. Varnish will dry to a scratch-resistant surface that is hard enough to rub down between applications.

Cellulose, better known as polyurethane varnish, is extremely durable and unaffected by water. It does not discolor when it is exposed to light. Spar varnish is available with chemicals added to make it resistant to salt water. Turpentine acts as a suitable thinner and cleaning agent to all varnishes.

When applying varnish to bare wood the pores should be filled and the surface should be as dust free as possible. At least two coats of varnish should be applied with rubbing between each coat done with fine steel wool or extra fine sandpaper. As you rub between coats you can feel the varnish finish smooth out as the bubbles and dust particles flatten. It is wise to allow plenty of drying time for a hard-finish coat; the harder the varnish surface the easier it is to rub between coats. Varnish is sold as high gloss, satin finish, or flat finish.

Lacquer

Lacquer is an excellent finish for it tends to dry fast and does not conceal the wood color. It can be identified by its bananalike odor. Lacquers are produced to be brushed or sprayed on. The quick drying is due to lacquer being applied in very thin coats. When lacquer is brushed on, it takes a longer drying period than spraying. Brush-type lacquer has a heavier consistency than the spray-type lacquer; therefore, it has a longer drying time.

Once the work is sanded to a smooth surface and stained, apply the first coat by brushing or spraying. A good spray job should have at least 3 to 4 light coats. Rubbing between each coat is not essential, for lacquer tends to dissolve into lacquer, leaving a smooth surface. Care must be taken in using a spray gun, for heavy spraying causes the lacquer to run and it is almost impossible to lift the runs. Lacquer should be thinned only with lacquer thinner and no other solvent.

To brush on lacquer apply the first coat as evenly as possible in the direction of the wood grain. After an overnight drying period, you can apply the second coat.

After your final application has dried for 36 hours you may find some imperfections in the form of uneven surface, dust particles, and small pits. These can be taken out easily by rubbing the surface down with wax imbedded into the steel wool pad. All safety rules for applying a combustible finish should be followed carefully when working with lacquer.

Finishing Oil

Finishing wood with oil is one of the oldest and best-known methods to date. It is easy to apply and maintain. A wood surface finished with oil will tend to dry out in time and can be easily revived with one new application of oil. If the surface is dirty all that is necessary is to wipe it down with turpentine or rub the dirt spots with steel wool.

Linseed oil is possibly the best type of oil finish to use, for it tends to last longer than other brands. When working with linseed oil you should use boiled linseed oil diluted to one part oil to one part turpentine or the formula may be adjusted to your taste.

The project should be sanded to a smooth surface with dust thoroughly removed. Wipe or brush the oil on generously with a clean cloth, allowing the oil to saturate the wood; if dull spots appear add more oil. When the wood cannot absorb any more oil wipe off the excess with a clean cloth. Begin to rub the surface down with a lint-free cloth made into the form of a pad. This will produce a satin finish. The key to working with oil is that one must rub hard enough with the heel of the hand to produce heat. After drying for 24 hours the same steps should be repeated exactly for four to six times to produce a beautiful satin finish.

Pumice

Pumice is a light, porous material obtained from volcanic lava. It acts as a sharp cutting material which smooths and polishes by causing fine, hairlike scratches. Pumice, which is available in powdered form, is used with oil, water, or paraffin to produce a very smooth finished surface.

A light film of oil or lubricant is applied to a cloth pad with pumice sprinkled over it. Rub the pumice in the direction of the grain until you reach a smooth finished surface.

Wax

Paste wax adds protection and life to the final finished surface by producing a tough film on the surface. The film protects the surface by making it water repellent and abrasion resistant. Some waxes require a damp cloth as an applicator. When applying the wax one should work in an area of approximately 3 square feet (.28 square m) at a time. The paste should be applied in an even layer. After its recommended drying time it should be buffed thoroughly. Polish the adjacent area, making sure to blend the entire finish so there are no bare spots.

MAKING CUSHIONS

Years ago cushions were filled with such material as goose and duck down or feathers. Today a multitude of new fibers is being used, the most popular being foam fillings—polyurethane foam and polyfoam.

Cushions that are squared-off and firm are usually stuffed with one to three layers of foam block depending upon your taste in comfort. The foam block can be purchased by the square foot and its thickness increases by 1-inch (2.5-cm) gradations.

It is more expensive to purchase a foam rubber block than a polyfoam block. Foam rubber is of a better quality for it weighs more, has more durability, and will not break down after repeated use.

Polyfoam and foam rubber are available in a number of grades of firmness ranging from supersoft to dense.

Usually cushions are fabricated with two different densities of foam. A common cushion for a seat may have a dense or medium foam core along with two outer layers of soft to supersoft foam. A common back cushion has a medium density for the center layer while the outer layers are soft to supersoft in density depending upon your comfort requirements.

Foam is simple to work with as it can be cut with a band saw, scissors, or a serrated bread knife. Cutting is easier if the knife or scissors are dipped into warm water or sprayed with silicone. Flat stock or small pieces of foam can be glued together with a rubber adhesive purchased at a fabric or upholstery shop.

Follow the step-by-step procedures coupled with the detailed drawings as a helpful guide in making the two types of cushions.

FINISHED KNIFE-EDGE CUSHION

MAKING A KNIFE-EDGE CUSHION

1. Cut two equal pieces of fabric then put the right sides together. If a zipper is to be used for the opening be sure to sew it into the two pieces first, using the manufacturer's directions on the package.

STEP 1.

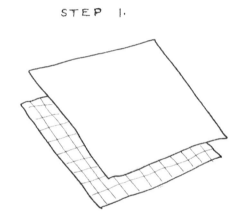

2. Sew the two equal pieces of fabric together along three sides and slightly around the corners of the fourth side. Make seam approximately 5/8 inch (16 mm) in from the edges.

STEP 2.

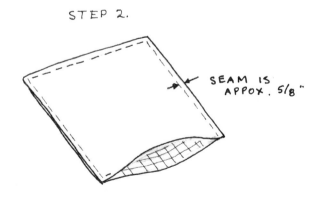

SEAM IS APPOX. 5/8"

3. Grade extra seam allowance then reverse the cover right-side-out and stuff with foam pad.

STEP 3.

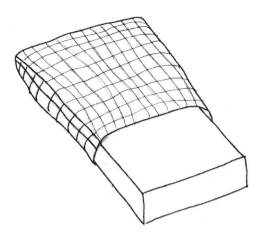

1. Cut out the top, bottom, and four side panels leaving enough material for approximately a 5/8" (16 mm) seam. If the opening panel is to have a zipper installed, allow an additional 1/2" (12.7 mm) for each side of the zipper.

2. If a zipper is to be used for the opening, sew it into one of the side panels following the manufacturer's instructions on the package. If a zipper is not to be used, plan to leave an opening in the panel.

4. If the opening is not to have a zipper it can be closed by sewing with an overcast stitch.

STEP 4.

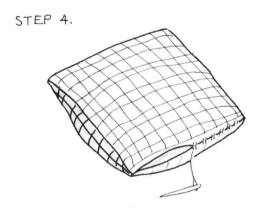

STEP 1, 2.

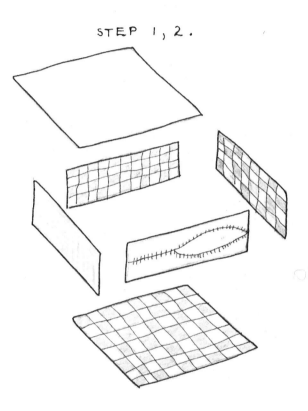

MAKING A BOX CUSHION

Unlike the simple knife-edge cushion which consists of only two pieces of fabric, the more difficult box cushion has six fabric pieces: the top, bottom, and four side panels. The side panels give the cushion its box shape.

FINISHED BOX EDGE CUSHION

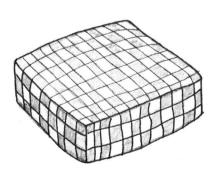

3. Align the fabric of the four side panels so that the finished material is facing in, then sew the ends together allowing approximately ⅝″ (16 mm) seams.

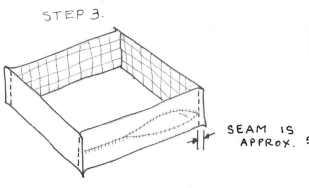

STEP 3.

SEAM IS APPROX. ⅝″

5. Reverse the fabric cover right-side-out and then stuff with foam padding wrapped with one layer of batting.

STEP 5.

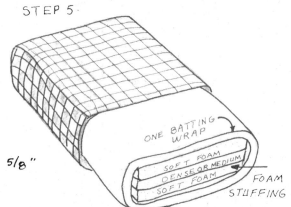

ONE BATTING WRAP

SOFT FOAM
DENSE OR MEDIUM
SOFT FOAM

FOAM STUFFING

COMMON SEAT CUSHION ARRANGEMENT.

4. Sew the top and bottom fabric pieces to the four side panels and then grade off excess seam.

STEP 4.

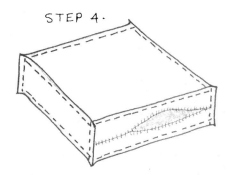

3 furniture projects

ARMLESS
COUCH, LOVE SEAT AND CHAIR.

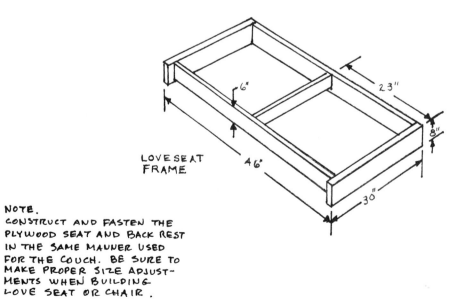

LOVE SEAT
FRAME

6"

23"

8"

46"

30"

NOTE.
CONSTRUCT AND FASTEN THE
PLYWOOD SEAT AND BACK REST
IN THE SAME MANNER USED
FOR THE COUCH. BE SURE TO
MAKE PROPER SIZE ADJUST-
MENTS WHEN BUILDING
LOVE SEAT OR CHAIR.

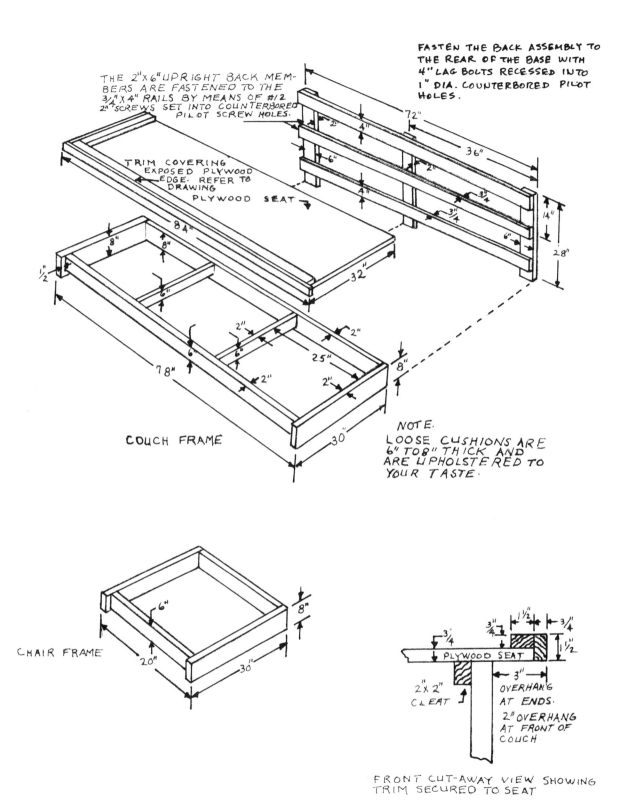

THE 2"x6" UPRIGHT BACK MEMBERS ARE FASTENED TO THE 3/4"x4" RAILS BY MEANS OF #12 2 1/4" SCREWS SET INTO COUNTERBORED PILOT SCREW HOLES.

FASTEN THE BACK ASSEMBLY TO THE REAR OF THE BASE WITH 4" LAG BOLTS RECESSED INTO 1" DIA. COUNTERBORED PILOT HOLES.

TRIM COVERING EXPOSED PLYWOOD EDGE. REFER TO DRAWING

PLYWOOD SEAT

COUCH FRAME

NOTE.
LOOSE CUSHIONS ARE 6" TO 8" THICK AND ARE UPHOLSTERED TO YOUR TASTE.

CHAIR FRAME

PLYWOOD SEAT

2"x2" CLEAT

OVERHANG AT ENDS.

2" OVERHANG AT FRONT OF COUCH

FRONT CUT-AWAY VIEW SHOWING TRIM SECURED TO SEAT

ARMLESS
COUCH, LOVE SEAT AND CHAIR.

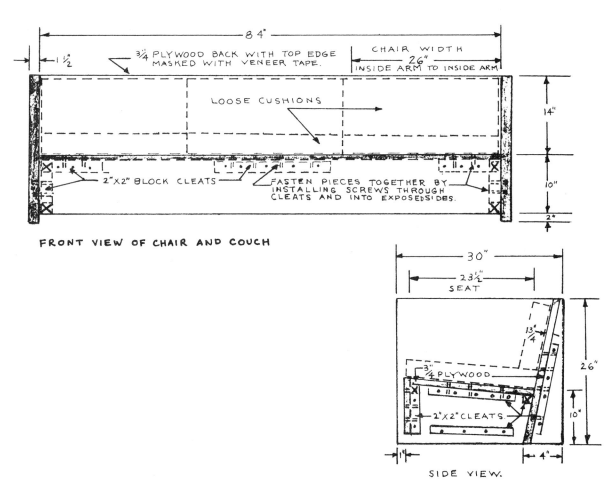

84"

1½"

3/4 PLYWOOD BACK WITH TOP EDGE MASKED WITH VENEER TAPE.

CHAIR WIDTH
26"
INSIDE ARM TO INSIDE ARM

LOOSE CUSHIONS

14"

2"X2" BLOCK CLEATS

FASTEN PIECES TOGETHER BY INSTALLING SCREWS THROUGH CLEATS AND INTO EXPOSED SIDES.

10"

2"

FRONT VIEW OF CHAIR AND COUCH

30"

23½"
SEAT

13/4"

3/4" PLYWOOD

26"

2"X2" CLEATS.

10"

1"

4"

SIDE VIEW.

MATCHING CHAIR AND COUCH

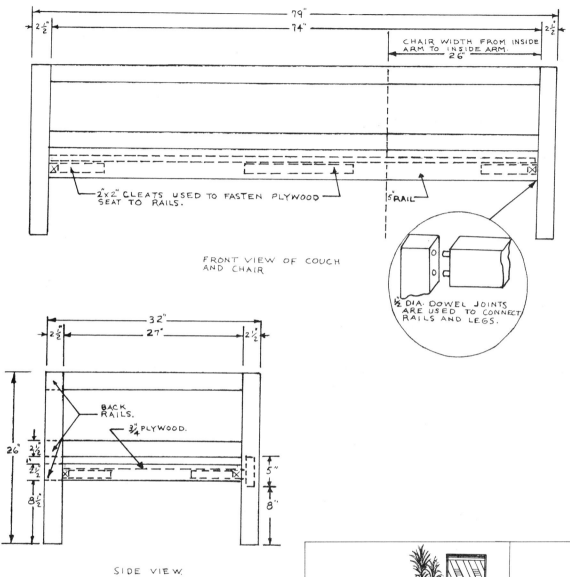

79"

74"

2½" 2½"

CHAIR WIDTH FROM INSIDE
ARM TO INSIDE ARM.
26"

2"x2" CLEATS USED TO FASTEN PLYWOOD
SEAT TO RAILS.

5" RAIL

FRONT VIEW OF COUCH
AND CHAIR

½" DIA. DOWEL JOINTS
ARE USED TO CONNECT
RAILS AND LEGS.

32"

27"

2½" 2½"

BACK
RAILS.

¾" PLYWOOD.

26"

2½"
2½"

5"

8½"

8"

SIDE VIEW.

COUCH/BED AND MATCHING CHAIR

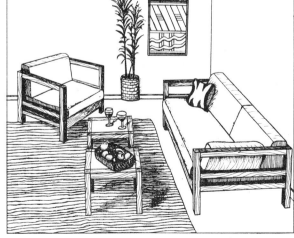

PARSONS TABLES

COFFEE TABLE
16"H X 36"W X 36"D

MAKE THESE VARIOUS SIZE
PARSONS TABLES

COFFEE TABLE
16"H X 54"W X 28"D

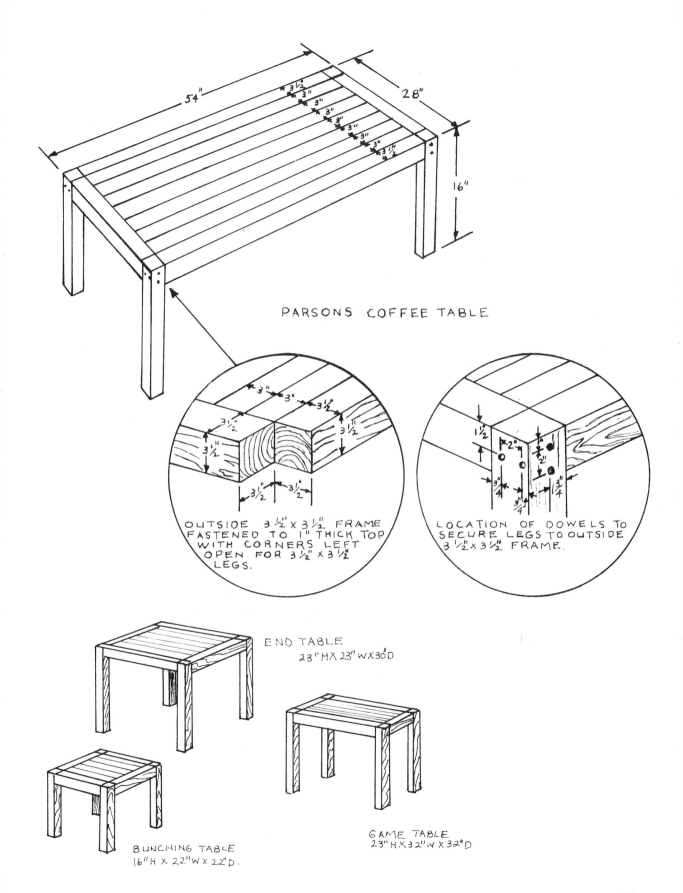

54"

28"

3½"
3"
3"
3"
3"
3"
3½"

16"

PARSONS COFFEE TABLE

3"
3"
3½"
3½"
3½"
3½"
3½"
3½"

OUTSIDE 3½" X 3½" FRAME
FASTENED TO 1" THICK TOP
WITH CORNERS LEFT
OPEN FOR 3½" X 3½"
LEGS.

1½"
2"
2"
3"/4
3"/4
3"/4
3"/4

LOCATION OF DOWELS TO
SECURE LEGS TO OUTSIDE
3½" X 3½" FRAME.

END TABLE
23"H X 23"W X 30"D

BUNCHING TABLE
16"H X 22"W X 22"D.

GAME TABLE
23"H X 32"W X 32"D

39

SET OF LIVING ROOM TABLES

END TABLE
20" H. X 20" W X 28" D.

COFFEE TABLE
16" H X 54" W X 28" D

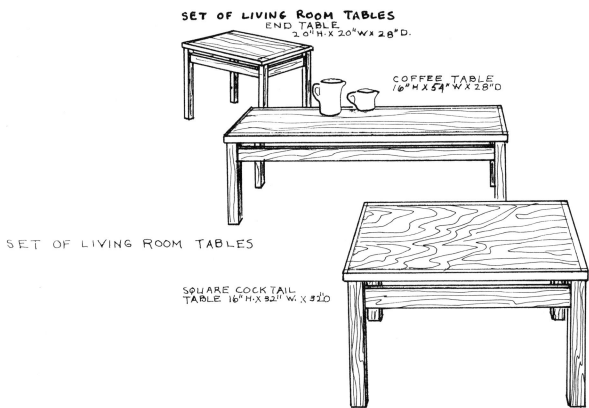

SET OF LIVING ROOM TABLES

SQUARE COCKTAIL
TABLE 16" H. X 32" W. X 32" D.

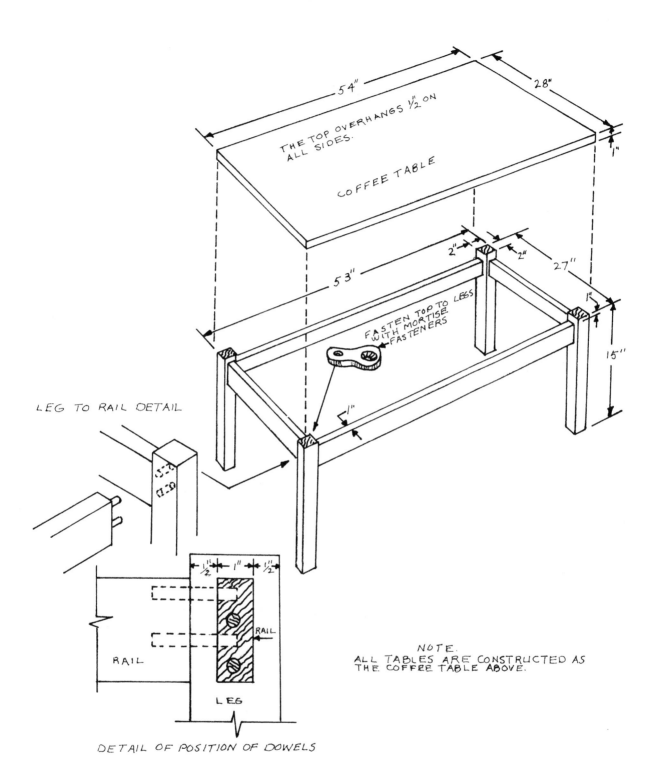

54"

28"

THE TOP OVERHANGS ½" ON ALL SIDES.

COFFEE TABLE

1"

53"

2"   2"

27"

FASTEN TOP TO LEGS WITH MORTISE FASTENERS

1"

15"

1"

LEG TO RAIL DETAIL

DETAIL OF POSITION OF DOWELS

RAIL

RAIL

LEG

½" 1" ½"

NOTE.
ALL TABLES ARE CONSTRUCTED AS THE COFFEE TABLE ABOVE.

COFFEE TABLE

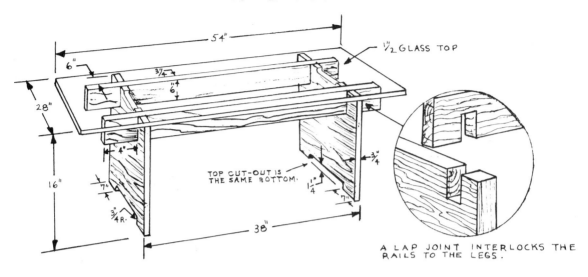

54"

6"

28"

3/4"

6"

16"

4"

7"

3/4 R.

38"

TOP CUT-OUT IS
THE SAME BOTTOM.

1/4"

7"

1/2" GLASS TOP

3/4"

A LAP JOINT INTERLOCKS THE
RAILS TO THE LEGS.

GLASS TOP TABLES

CORNER TABLE
16"H x 22"W x 22"D

SQUARE COCKTAIL TABLE
16"H x 36"W x 36"D.

COFFEE TABLE
16"H x 54"W x 28"D.

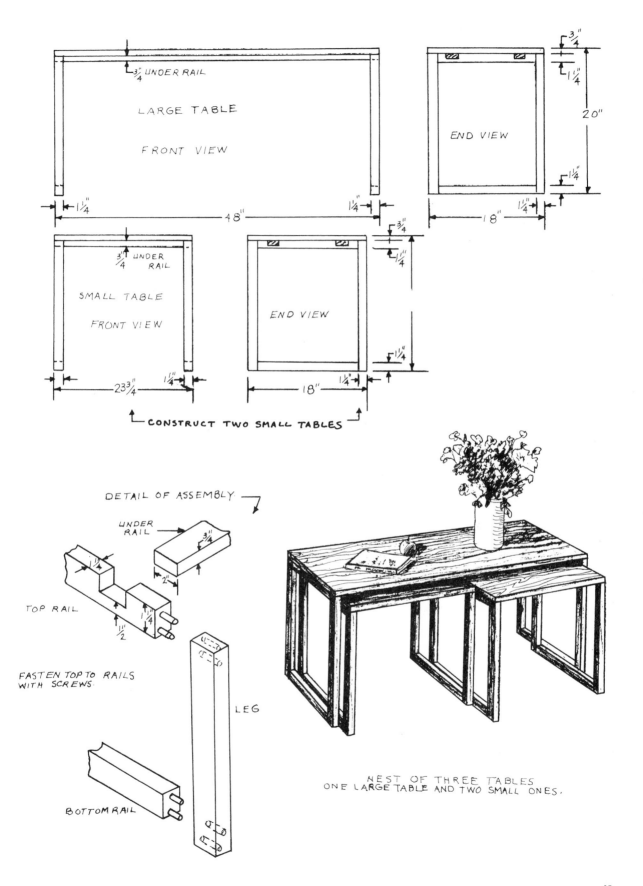

3/4" UNDER RAIL

LARGE TABLE

FRONT VIEW

END VIEW

3/4"

1 1/4"

20"

1 1/4"

1 1/4"

1 1/4"

48"

1 1/4"

18"

3/4" UNDER RAIL

SMALL TABLE

FRONT VIEW

END VIEW

3/4"

1 1/4"

23 3/4"

1 1/4"

1 1/4"

18"

1 1/4"

CONSTRUCT TWO SMALL TABLES

DETAIL OF ASSEMBLY

UNDER RAIL

3/4"

2"

TOP RAIL

1 1/4"

1 1/4"

1/2"

FASTEN TOP TO RAILS WITH SCREWS.

LEG

BOTTOM RAIL

NEST OF THREE TABLES
ONE LARGE TABLE AND TWO SMALL ONES.

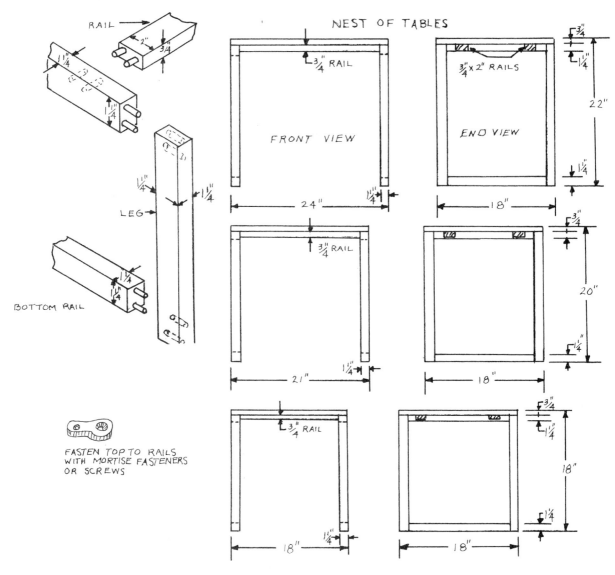

RAIL

2"

3/4

1 1/4

1 1/4

LEG

1 1/4

1 1/4

BOTTOM RAIL

1 1/4

1 1/4

3/4" RAIL

FRONT VIEW

3/4" x 2" RAILS

END VIEW

3/4

1 1/4

22"

1 1/4

24"

1 1/4

18"

3/4" RAIL

3/4

20"

1 1/4

21"

1 1/4

18"

FASTEN TOP TO RAILS
WITH MORTISE FASTENERS
OR SCREWS

3/4" RAIL

3/4

1 1/4

18"

18"

1 1/4

18"

18"

NEST OF THREE TABLES

BLOCK
COFFEE TABLE

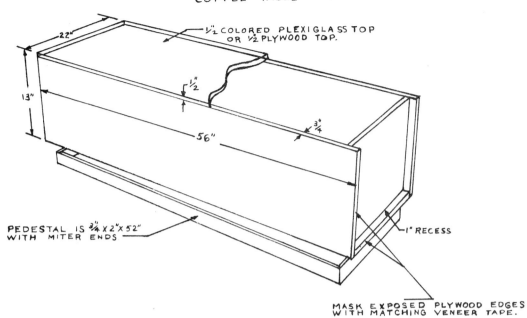

22"

½" COLORED PLEXIGLASS TOP
OR ½ PLYWOOD TOP.

13"

1½"

56"

¾"

PEDESTAL IS ¾"X2"X52"
WITH MITER ENDS

1" RECESS

MASK EXPOSED PLYWOOD EDGES
WITH MATCHING VENEER TAPE.

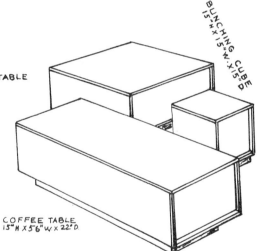

BUNCHING CUBE
15"W.X15"W.X15"D.

SQUARE COCKTAIL TABLE
15"H X 36" W X 36" D.

COFFEE TABLE
15" H X 56" W X 22"D.

BLOCK TABLES

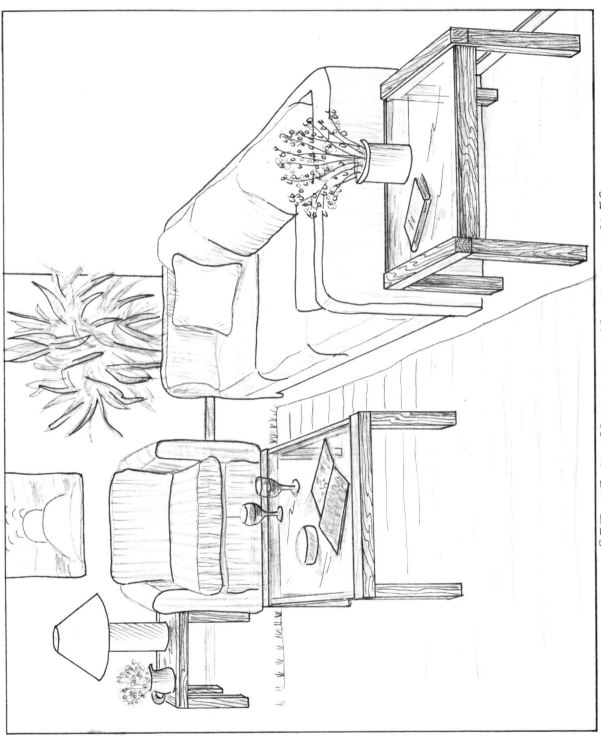

SET OF GLASS TOP LIVING ROOM TABLES

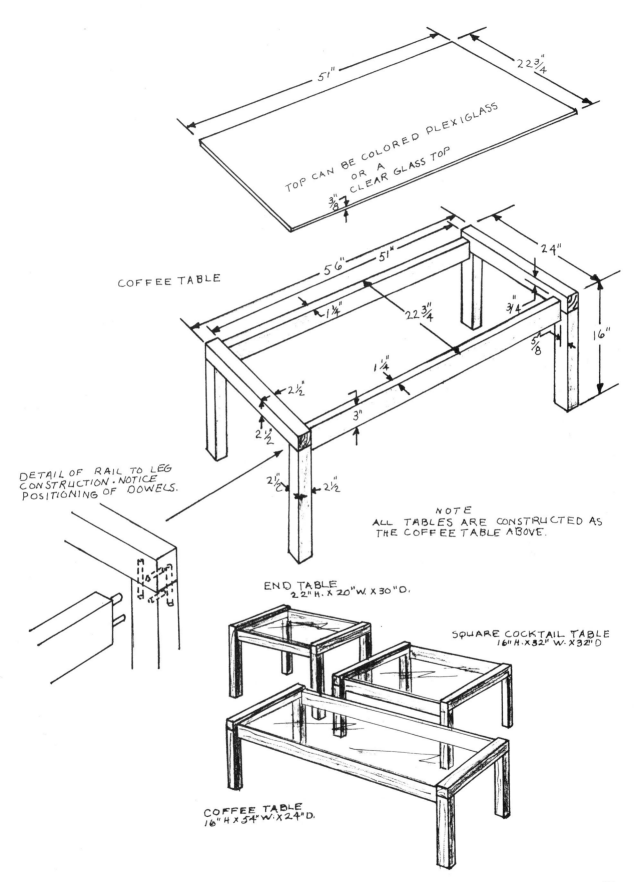

51"

22 3/4"

TOP CAN BE COLORED PLEXIGLASS
OR A
CLEAR GLASS TOP

3/8"

COFFEE TABLE

56" 51"

24"

1 1/4"

22 3/4"

3/4

16"

5/8

1 1/4"

2 1/2

3"

2 1/2

DETAIL OF RAIL TO LEG
CONSTRUCTION. NOTICE
POSITIONING OF DOWELS.

2 1/2
C

2 1/2

NOTE
ALL TABLES ARE CONSTRUCTED AS
THE COFFEE TABLE ABOVE.

END TABLE
22" H. X 20" W. X 30" D.

SQUARE COCKTAIL TABLE
16" H. X 32" W. X 32" D

COFFEE TABLE
16" H X 54" W. X 24" D.

SET OF LIVING ROOM TABLES
COCKTAIL TABLE ALONG WITH END TABLE/PLANT STAND.

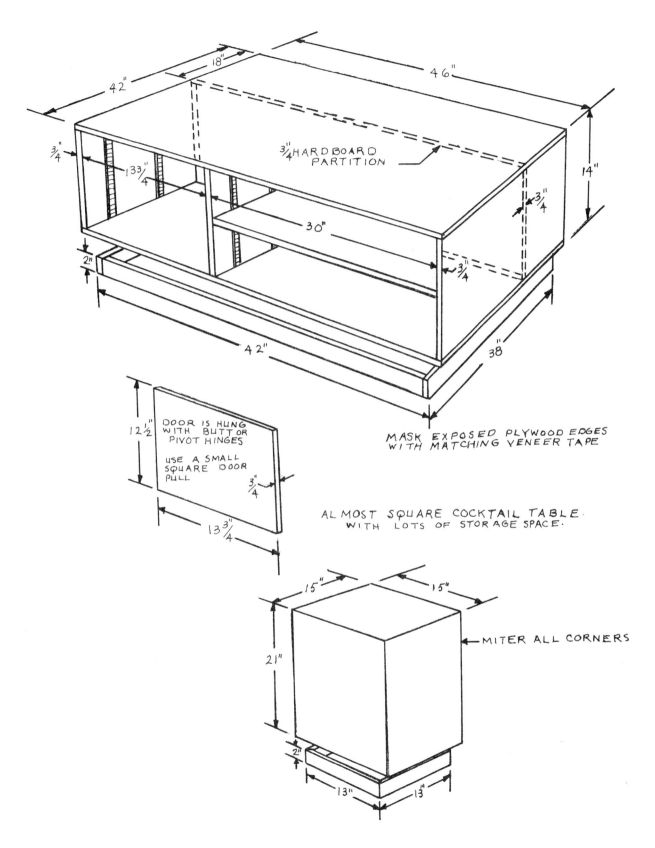

42"

18"

46"

3/4"

14"

13 3/4"

3/4" HARDBOARD PARTITION

30"

3/4"

2"

3/4"

42"

38"

MASK EXPOSED PLYWOOD EDGES
WITH MATCHING VENEER TAPE

12 1/2"

DOOR IS HUNG
WITH BUTT OR
PIVOT HINGES

USE A SMALL
SQUARE DOOR
PULL

3/4"

13 3/4"

ALMOST SQUARE COCKTAIL TABLE
WITH LOTS OF STORAGE SPACE.

15"

15"

MITER ALL CORNERS

21"

2"

13"

13"

END TABLE OR PLANT STAND

SOFA TABLE

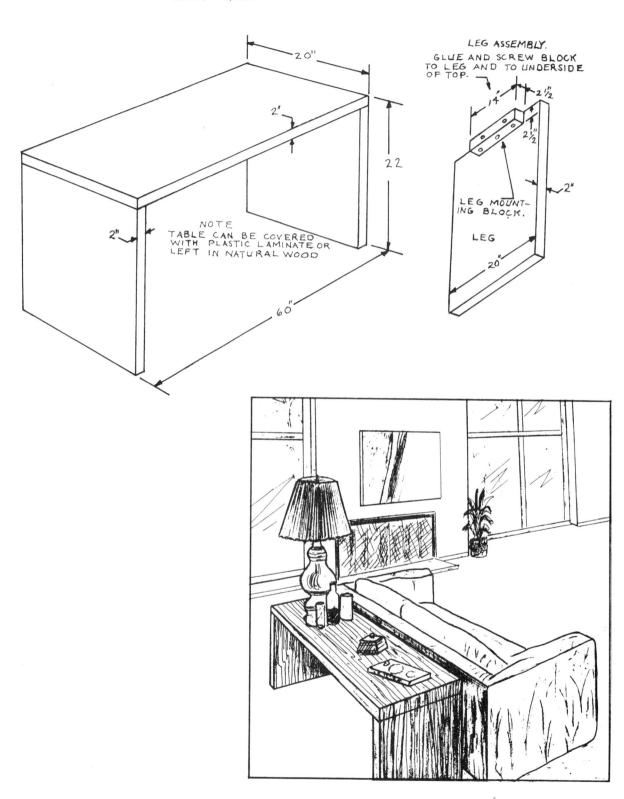

20"

2"

22

2"

NOTE
TABLE CAN BE COVERED
WITH PLASTIC LAMINATE OR
LEFT IN NATURAL WOOD

60"

LEG ASSEMBLY.
GLUE AND SCREW BLOCK
TO LEG AND TO UNDERSIDE
OF TOP.

14"

2 1/2"

2 1/2"

2"

LEG MOUNT-
ING BLOCK.

LEG

20"

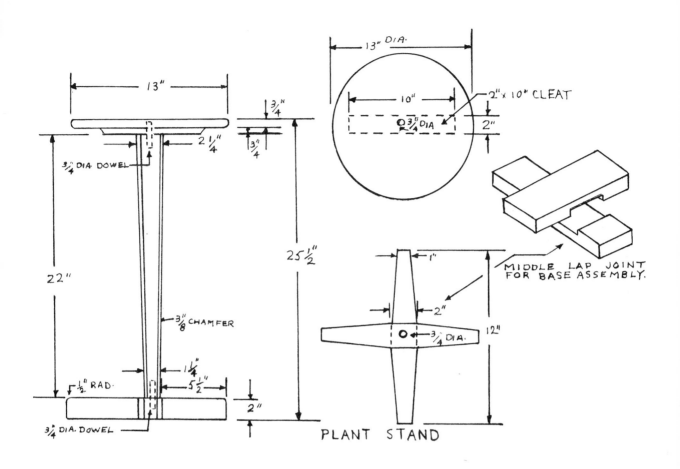

13"

3/4"

2 1/4"

3/4"

3/4 DIA DOWEL

22"

3/8" CHAMFER

1/2" RAD.

1 1/4"

5 1/2"

2"

3/4 DIA. DOWEL

25 1/2"

13" DIA.

10"

2" x 10" CLEAT

3/4" DIA

2"

MIDDLE LAP JOINT
FOR BASE ASSEMBLY.

1"

2"

3/4" DIA.

12"

PLANT STAND

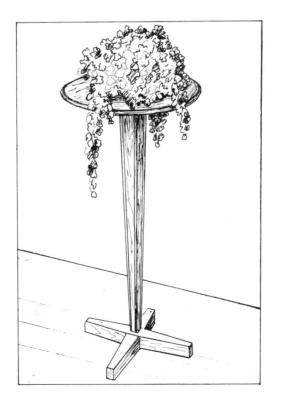

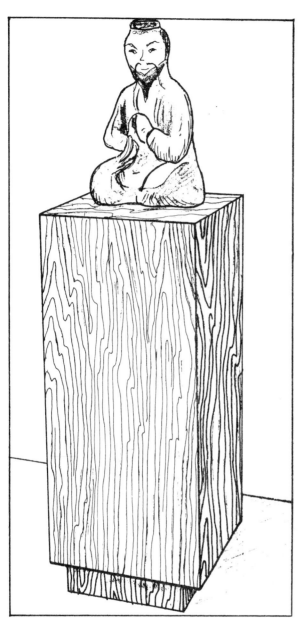

ART/PLANT PEDESTAL

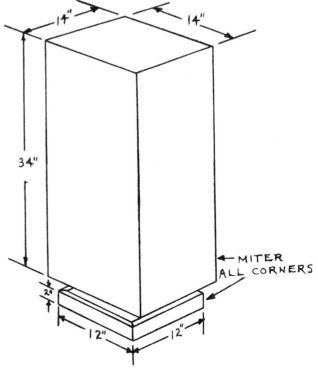

14"

14"

34"

MITER
ALL CORNERS

2"

12"

12"

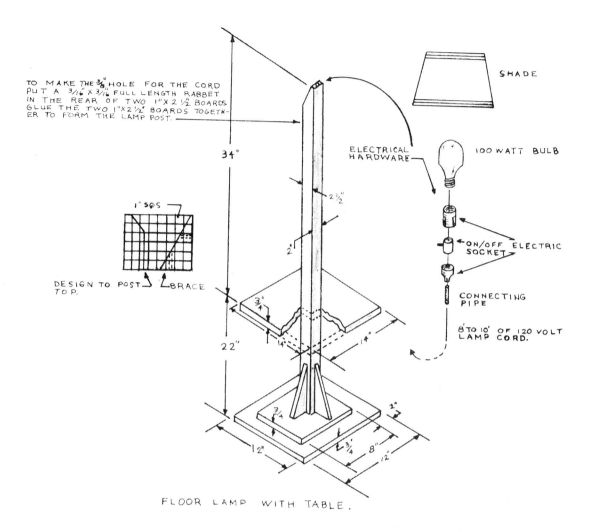

TO MAKE THE 3/8" HOLE FOR THE CORD
PUT A 3/16" X 3/16" FULL LENGTH RABBET
IN THE REAR OF TWO 1" X 2 1/2 BOARDS
GLUE THE TWO 1" X 2 1/2" BOARDS TOGETH-
ER TO FORM THE LAMP POST.

SHADE

ELECTRICAL
HARDWARE

100 WATT BULB

ON/OFF ELECTRIC
SOCKET

CONNECTING
PIPE

8' TO 10' OF 120 VOLT
LAMP CORD.

1" SQS

DESIGN TO POST
TOP.
BRACE

34"

2 1/2"

2'

22"

3/4"

14"

14"

12"

3/4"

3/4"

8"

12"

1"

FLOOR LAMP WITH TABLE.

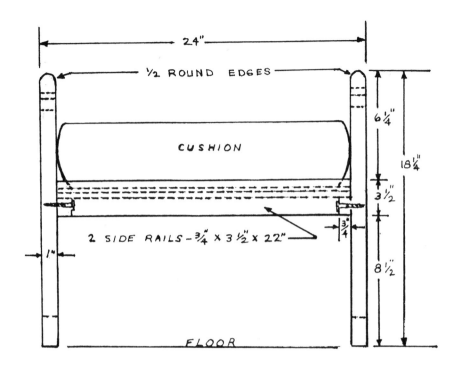

24"

½ ROUND EDGES

6¼"

18¼"

CUSHION

3½"

¾"

2 SIDE RAILS - ¾" X 3½" X 22"

8½"

1"

FLOOR

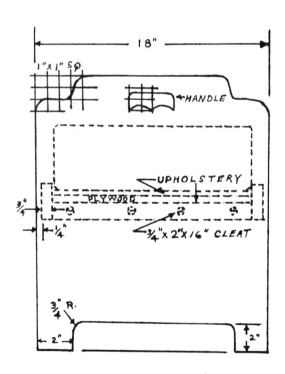

18"

1" X 1" SQ.

HANDLE

UPHOLSTERY

¾"

PLYWOOD

¾" X 2" X 16" CLEAT

¼"

¾" R.

2"

2"

FOOT REST

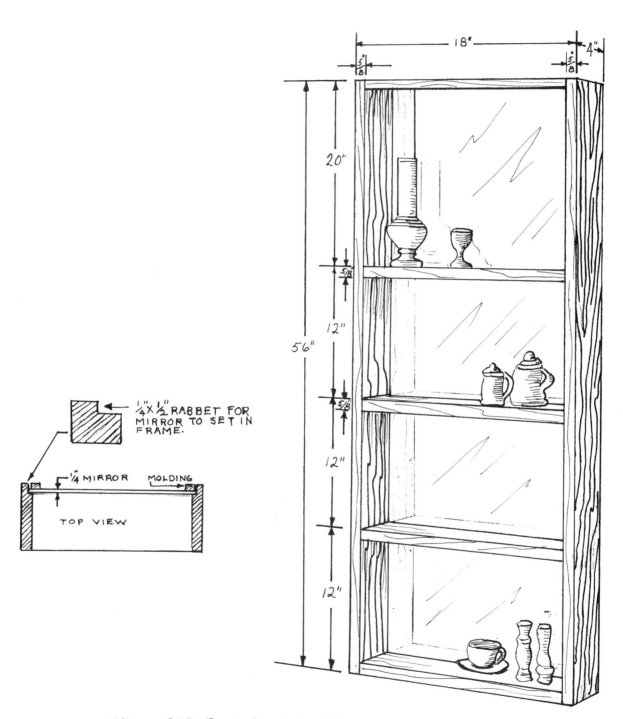

1"⁄4 X 1⁄2" RABBET FOR MIRROR TO SET IN FRAME.

1⁄4 MIRROR   MOLDING

TOP VIEW

18"   4"

5⁄8   5⁄8

20"

5⁄8

56"   12"

5⁄8

12"

12"

WALL SHELF WITH MIRROR

HUTCH

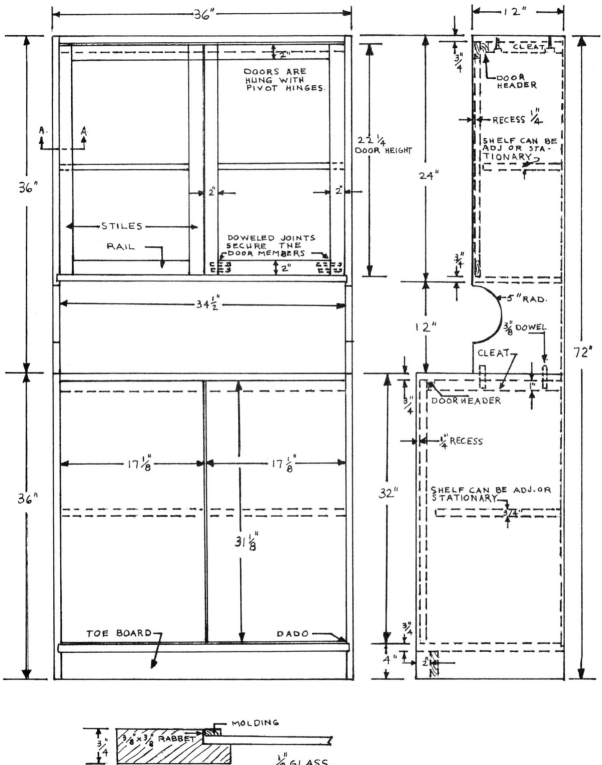

36"

2"

DOORS ARE
HUNG WITH
PIVOT HINGES.

22¼"
DOOR HEIGHT

A.   A

36"

2"   2"

STILES

RAIL

DOWELED JOINTS
SECURE THE
DOOR MEMBERS

2"

34½"

17⅛"   17⅛"

31⅛"

36"

TOE BOARD   DADO

12"

CLEAT

¾"

DOOR
HEADER

RECESS 1¼"

SHELF CAN BE
ADJ OR STA-
TIONARY?

24"

¾"

5" RAD.

3/8" DOWEL

CLEAT

12"

DOOR HEADER

¾"

1"

1¼" RECESS

SHELF CAN BE ADJ. OR
STATIONARY

32"

¾"

72"

¾"

4"   2"

MOLDING

¾"   ⅜" × ⅜" RABBET

⅛" GLASS

SECTION·A·A   2"

BUFFET

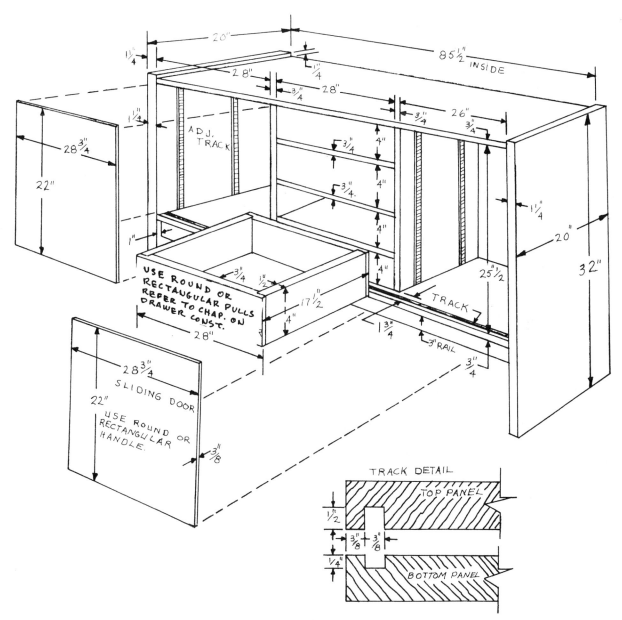

20"

1¼"

85½" INSIDE

28"

1¼"

¾"

28"

¾"

26"

¾"

1¼"

28¾"

ADJ.
TRACK

¾"

4"

¾"

4"

22"

¾"

4"

20"

1"

4"

USE ROUND OR
RECTANGULAR PULLS
REFER TO CHAP. ON
DRAWER CONST.

¾"

½"

17½"

25½"

TRACK

4"

28¾"

SLIDING DOOR

28"

1¾"

3" RAIL

¾"

22"

USE ROUND OR
RECTANGULAR
HANDLE.

32"

4"

3"
8

TRACK DETAIL

TOP PANEL

½"

3"
8

3"
8

¼"

BOTTOM PANEL

TRACKS ARE GROOVED WITH A ROUTER OR
ON A TABLE SAW. GROOVE IS DEEPER IN TOP
PANEL TO ALLOW DOORS TO BE INSTALLED.

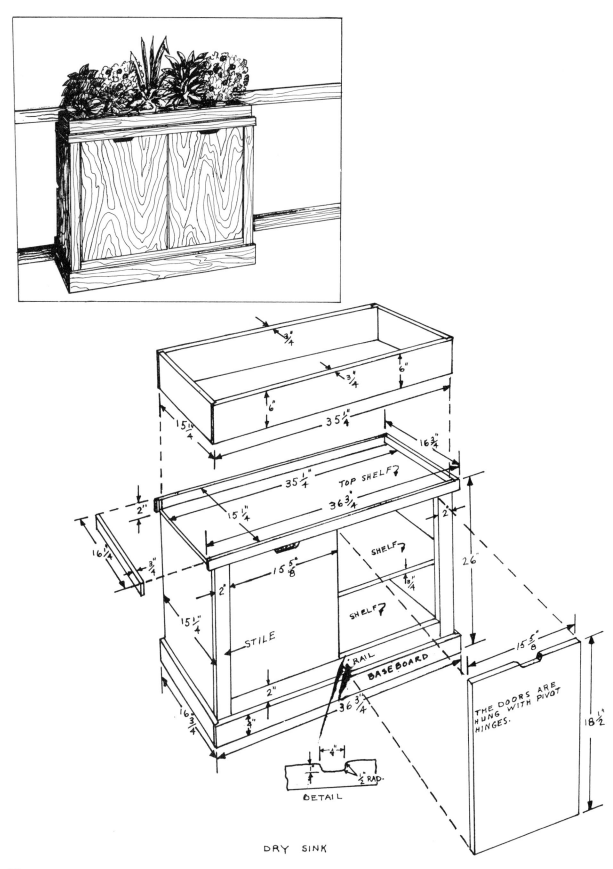

DRY SINK

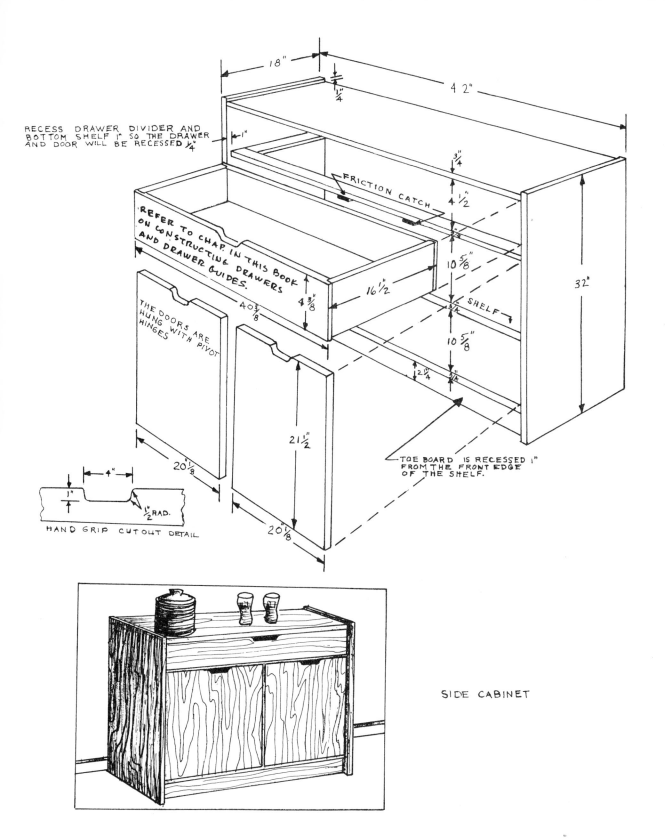

18"

4 2"

1/4"

RECESS DRAWER DIVIDER AND
BOTTOM SHELF 1" SO THE DRAWER
AND DOOR WILL BE RECESSED 1/4"

1"

FRICTION CATCH

3/4"

4 1/2"

REFER TO CHAP. IN THIS BOOK
ON CONSTRUCTING DRAWERS
AND DRAWER GUIDES.

3/4"

10 5/8"

32"

16 1/2"

SHELF

4 3/8"

3/4"

THE DOORS ARE
HUNG WITH PIVOT
HINGES

40 3/8"

10 5/8"

12 1/4"

3/4"

21 1/2"

20 1/8"

TOE BOARD IS RECESSED 1"
FROM THE FRONT EDGE
OF THE SHELF.

4"

1"

1/2" RAD.

HAND GRIP CUTOUT DETAIL

20 1/8"

SIDE CABINET

CORNER CABINET

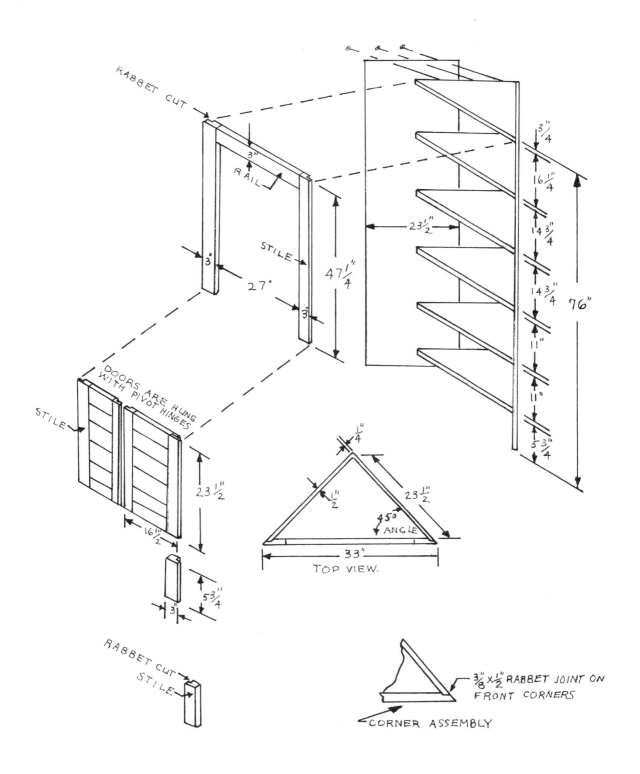

RABBET CUT

3"

RAIL

STILE

3"

27"

3"

47 1/4"

23 1/2"

3/4"

16 1/4"

14 3/4"

14 3/4"

11"

11"

5 3/4"

76"

DOORS ARE HUNG
WITH PIVOT HINGES

STILE

23 1/2"

16 1/2"

5 3/4"

3"

RABBET CUT
STILE

1/4"

1/2"

23 1/2"

45°
ANGLE

33"

TOP VIEW.

3/8" x 1/2" RABBET JOINT ON
FRONT CORNERS

CORNER ASSEMBLY

CORNER CABINET

SIDEBOARD

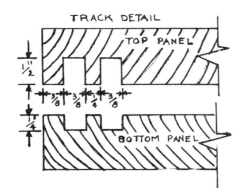

TRACK DETAIL

TOP PANEL

BOTTOM PANEL

TRACKS ARE GROOVED WITH A ROUTER OR
ON A TABLE SAW. GROOVES ARE DEEPER IN TOP
PANEL TO ALLOW DOORS TO BE INSTALLED.

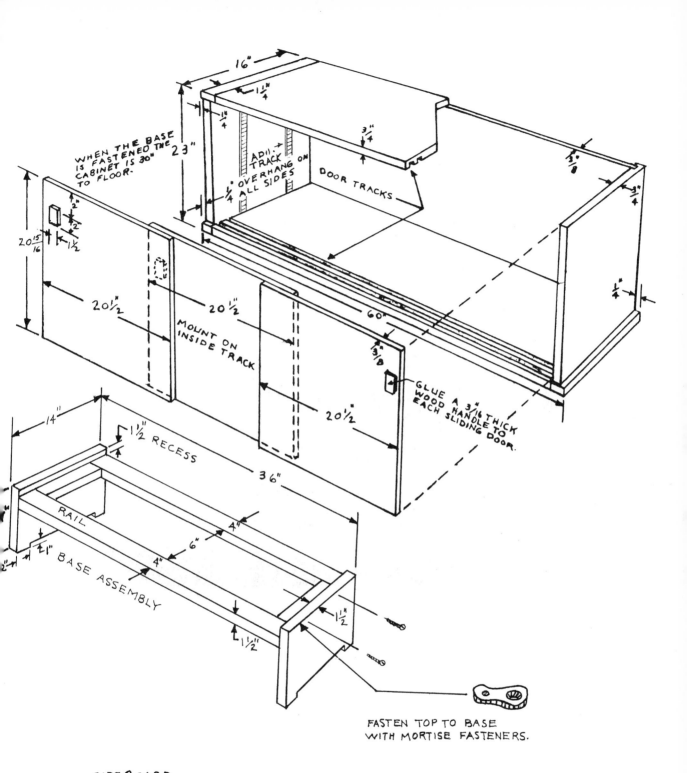

16"

1 1/4"

1/4"

WHEN THE BASE
IS FASTENED THE
CABINET IS 30"
TO FLOOR.

23"

ADD. TRACK

1/4" OVERHANG ON
ALL SIDES

DOOR TRACKS

3/4"

3/8"

3/4"

2"

2"

20 15/16"

1 1/2"

20 1/2"

20 1/2"

MOUNT ON
INSIDE TRACK

60"

1/4"

GLUE A 3/16" THICK
WOOD HANDLE TO
EACH SLIDING DOOR.

3/8"

20 1/2"

36"

14"

1 1/2" RECESS

RAIL

1"

BASE ASSEMBLY

4"

6"

4"

1 1/2"

1 1/2"

2"

FASTEN TOP TO BASE
WITH MORTISE FASTENERS.

SIDEBOARD
WITH THREE SLIDING DOORS

65

MATCHING SIDEBOARD AND HUTCH

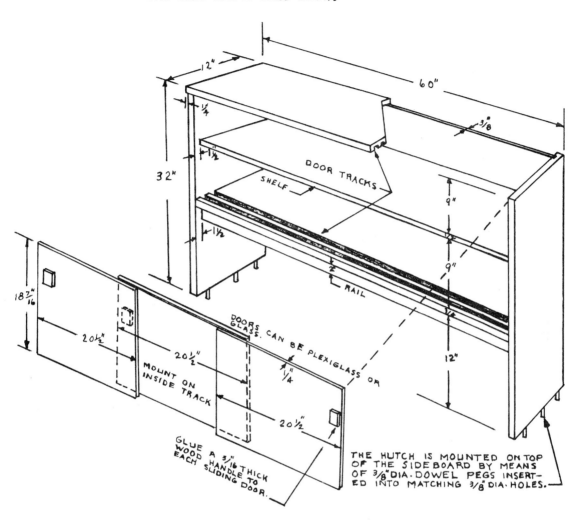

12"
60"
1/4
3/8
32"
DOOR TRACKS
9"
SHELF
1 1/2
9"
1 1/2
DOORS CAN BE PLEXIGLASS OR GLASS
RAIL
12"
18 7/16
20 1/2
20 1/2
1/4
MOUNT ON INSIDE TRACK
20 1/2

GLUE A 3/16" THICK WOOD HANDLE TO EACH SLIDING DOOR.

THE HUTCH IS MOUNTED ON TOP OF THE SIDEBOARD BY MEANS OF 3/8" DIA. DOWEL PEGS INSERTED INTO MATCHING 3/8" DIA. HOLES.

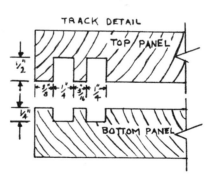

TRACK DETAIL

TOP PANEL

1/2"

3/8" 1/4" 3/16" 1/4"

1/4"

BOTTOM PANEL

TRACKS ARE GROOVED WITH A ROUTER OR ON A TABLE SAW. GROOVES ARE DEEPER IN TOP PANEL TO ALLOW DOORS TO BE INSTALLED.

ROUND DINING TABLE

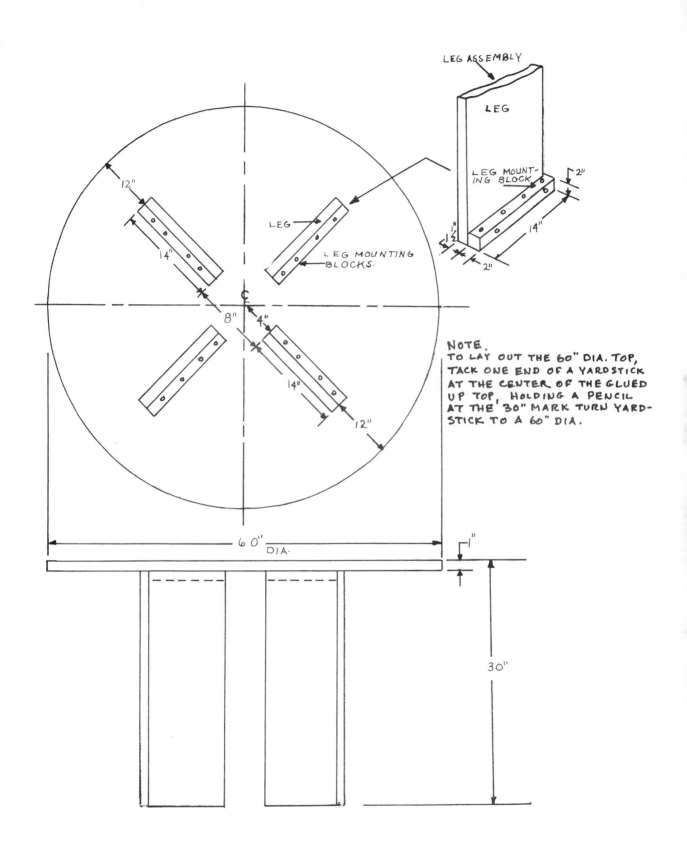

LEG ASSEMBLY

LEG

LEG MOUNTING BLOCK

2"

1"

2"

14"

12"

14"

LEG

LEG MOUNTING BLOCKS.

C

8" 4"

14"

12"

60" DIA.

1"

30"

NOTE.
TO LAY OUT THE 60" DIA. TOP,
TACK ONE END OF A YARDSTICK
AT THE CENTER OF THE GLUED
UP TOP, HOLDING A PENCIL
AT THE 30" MARK TURN YARD-
STICK TO A 60" DIA.

ROUND DINING TABLE

DINING TABLE
WITH CLEAN LINES AND GENEROUS SIZE

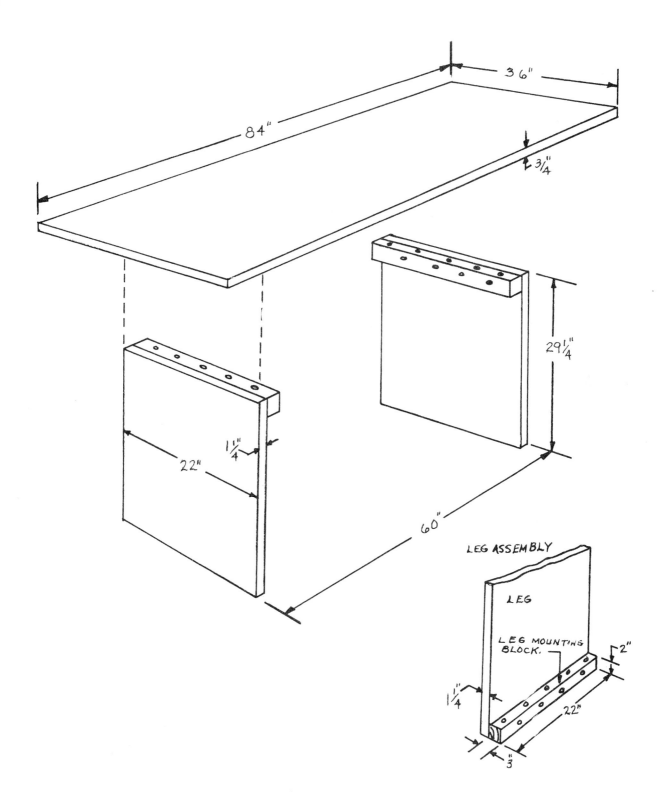

36"

84"

3 1/4"

29 1/4"

1 1/4"

22"

60"

LEG ASSEMBLY

LEG

LEG MOUNTING
BLOCK.

1 1/4"

22"

2"

3"

DINING TABLE
WITH CLEAN LINES AND GENEROUS SIZE.

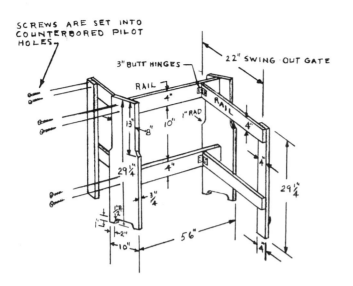

SCREWS ARE SET INTO
COUNTERBORED PILOT
HOLES

3" BUTT HINGES

22" SWING OUT GATE

RAIL

RAIL

4"

13"

8"

10"

1" RAD

4"

4"

29¼"

4"

4"

29¼"

3¼"

½"R

2"

1½"

2"

10"

56"

4"

ROUND GATE LEG TABLE

TWO DROP LEAVES
ARE 26" EACH THEY
ARE HINGED TO THE
UNDER SIDE OF THE
8" CENTER BOARD

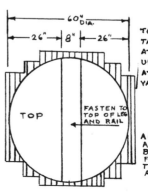

60" DIA.

26"

8"

26"

TOP

FASTEN TO
TOP OF LEG
AND RAIL

TO LAY OUT THE 60" DIA. TOP,
TACK ONE END OF A YARDSTICK
AT THE CENTER OF THE GLUED
UP STOCK, HOLDING A PENCIL
AT THE 30" MARK TURN THE
YARDSTICK.

AFTER THE TOP IS CUT TO
A 60" DIA. CUT AN 8" WIDE
BOARD FROM THE CENTER.
FASTEN THE 8" BOARD TO
THE TOP OF THE CROSS RAIL
AND LEGS.

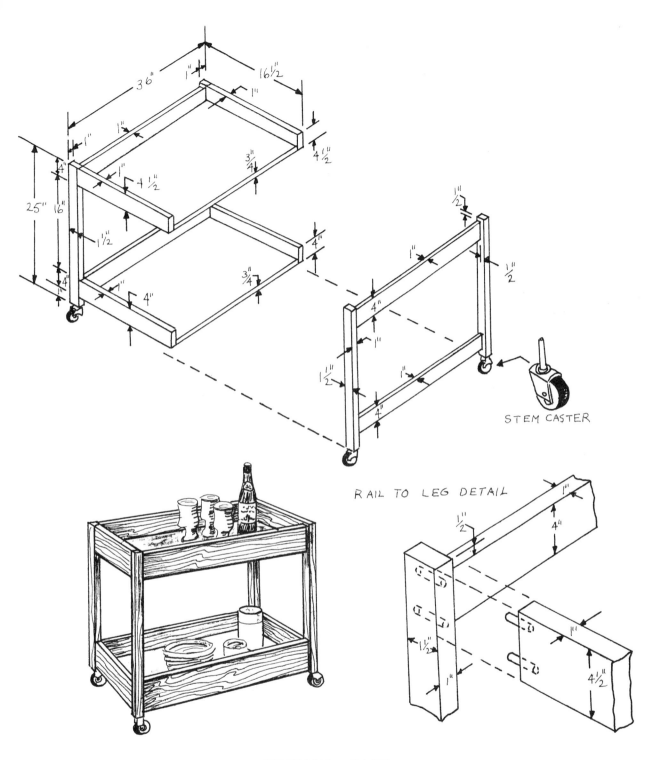

36"

16½"

1"

1"

1"

1"

25" 16"

4"

4"

1½"

4½"

3/4"

4"

4"

4"

3/4"

4"

4 1/2"

1/2"

1"

1½"

1"

4"

4"

1"

1½"

1"

4"

STEM CASTER

RAIL TO LEG DETAIL

1"

4"

1/2"

1½"

1"

1"

4½"

SERVING CART

DINING TABLE

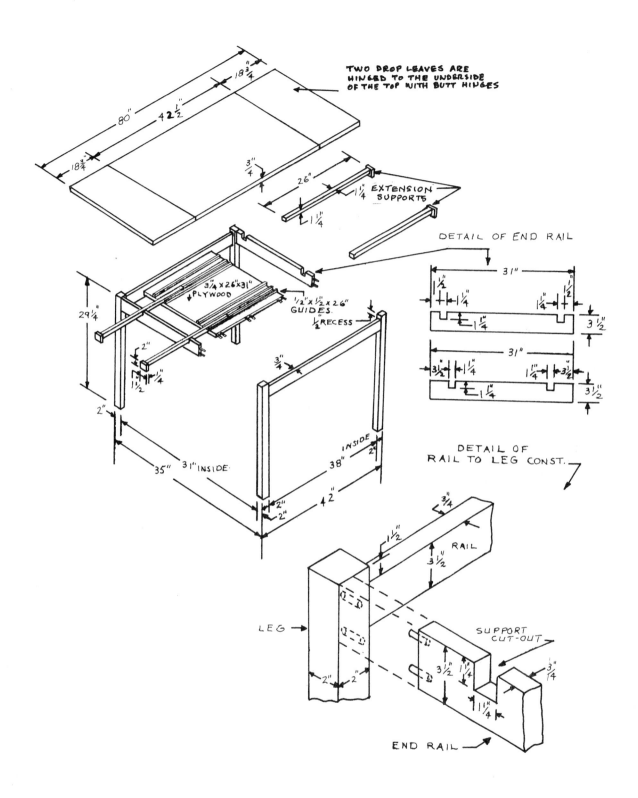

TWO DROP LEAVES ARE HINGED TO THE UNDERSIDE OF THE TOP WITH BUTT HINGES

EXTENSION SUPPORTS

DETAIL OF END RAIL

3/4 X 26" X 31" PLYWOOD

1/2"X 1 1/2"X 26" GUIDES.

1/2 RECESS

DETAIL OF RAIL TO LEG CONST.

RAIL

LEG

SUPPORT CUT-OUT

END RAIL

DINING TABLE

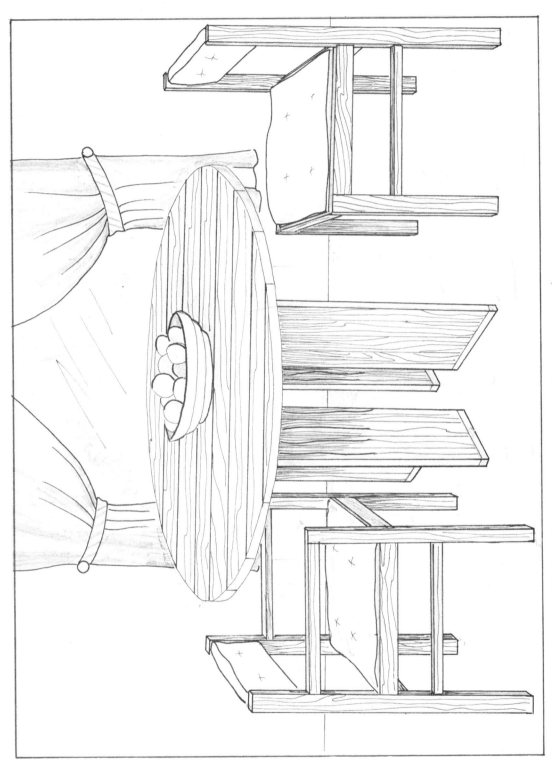

DINING CHAIRS

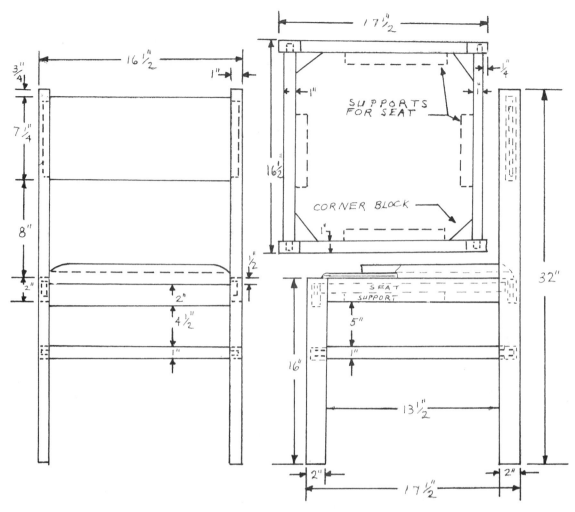

SUPPORTS FOR SEAT

CORNER BLOCK

SEAT SUPPORT

NOTE:
THE BACK REST AND SEAT
CAN BE UPHOLSTERED TO
YOUR CHOICE OR LEFT IN WOOD.

LEG AND RAIL DETAIL

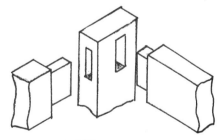

NOTE:
MORTISE AND TENON OR DOWEL
JOINTS CAN BE USED TO FASTEN
RAILS TO LEGS.

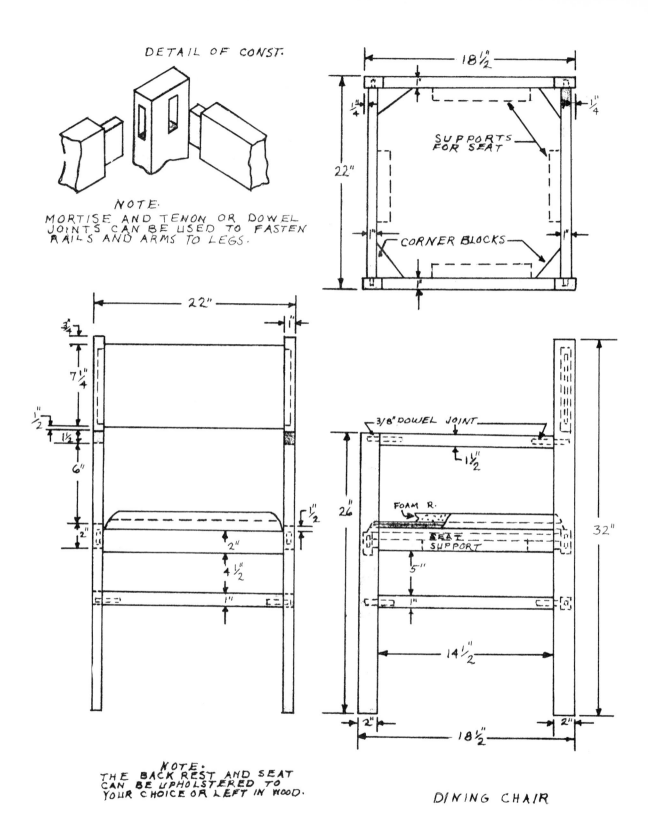

DETAIL OF CONST.

NOTE:
MORTISE AND TENON OR DOWEL
JOINTS CAN BE USED TO FASTEN
RAILS AND ARMS TO LEGS.

18 1/2"

22"

1/4"

1/4"

SUPPORTS
FOR SEAT

CORNER BLOCKS

1"

1"

1"

22"

1"

3/4"

7 1/4"

1/2"

1 1/2"

6"

1/2"

2"

2"

4 1/2"

1"

NOTE:
THE BACK REST AND SEAT
CAN BE UPHOLSTERED TO
YOUR CHOICE OR LEFT IN WOOD.

3/8" DOWEL JOINT

1 1/2"

FOAM R.

SEAT
SUPPORT

26"

5"

32"

1"

14 1/2"

2"

18 1/2"

2"

DINING CHAIR

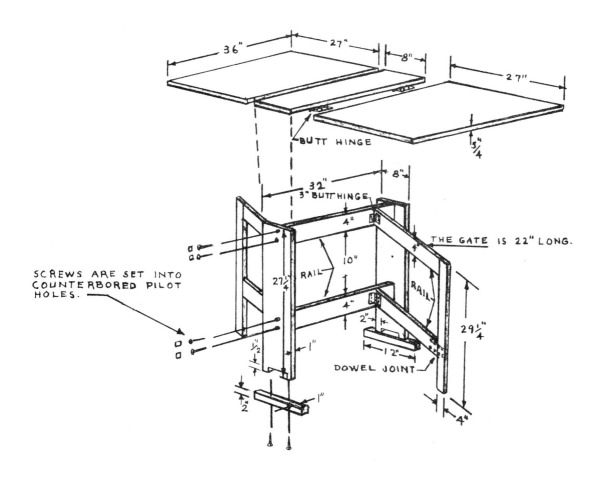

36"   27"   8"   27"

BUTT HINGE

5/4"

32"   8"

3" BUTT HINGE

4"

THE GATE IS 22" LONG.

10"

SCREWS ARE SET INTO
COUNTERBORED PILOT
HOLES.

27 1/4"   RAIL   RAIL

4"

29 1/4"

2"

1/2"   1"

12"

DOWEL JOINT

4"

1/2"   1"

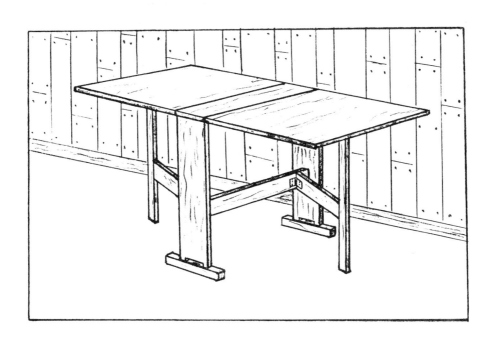

RECTANGULAR
GATE LEG TABLE

DINING ROOM TRESTLE TABLE

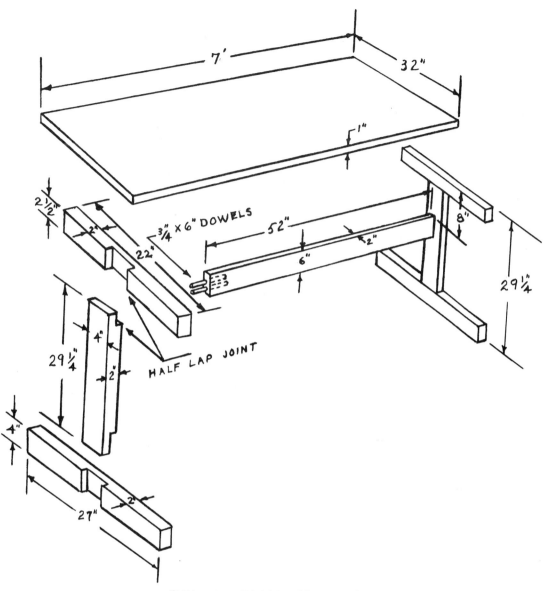

7'

32"

1"

2½"

2"

3/4" × 6" DOWELS

52"

8"

22"

2"

6"

29¼"

4"

2"

29¼"

HALF LAP JOINT

4"

27"

2"

DINING ROOM TRESTLE TABLE

KITCHEN WORK CENTER

DETAIL OF RAIL TO LEG
CONSTRUCTION. NOTICE
POSITIONING OF DOWEL JOINTS.

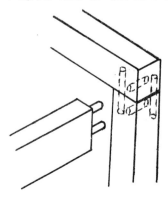

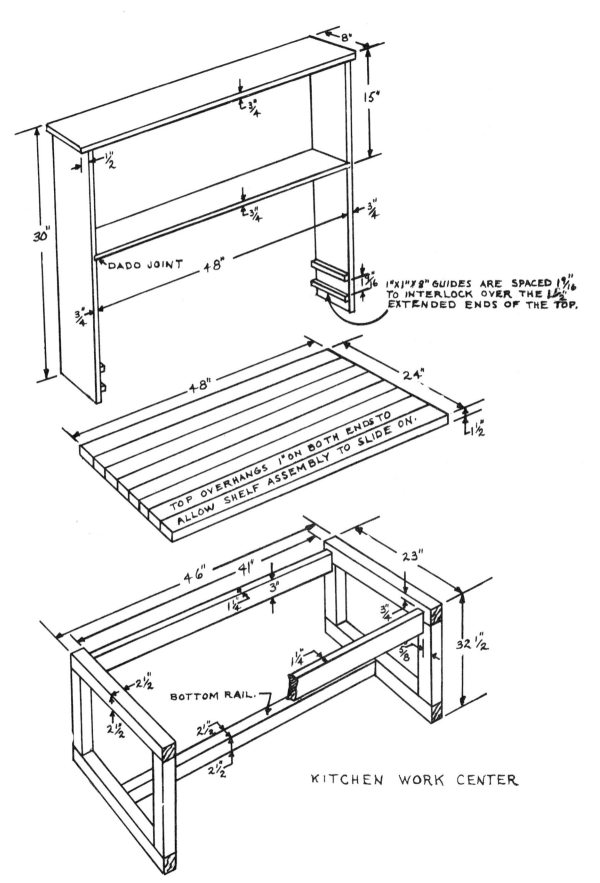

8"

15"

3/4"

1 1/2"

30"

3/4"

DADO JOINT   48"

3/4"

3/4"

1 9/16"

1"x1"x8" GUIDES ARE SPACED 1 9/16"
TO INTERLOCK OVER THE 1 1/2"
EXTENDED ENDS OF THE TOP.

24"

48"

1 1/2"

TOP OVERHANGS 1" ON BOTH ENDS TO
ALLOW SHELF ASSEMBLY TO SLIDE ON.

46"   41"   3"   23"

1 1/4"   3/4"

32 1/2"

1 1/4"   5/8"

2 1/2"

BOTTOM RAIL.

2 1/2"

2 1/2"

2 1/2"

KITCHEN WORK CENTER

KITCHEN DESK-CUPBOARD.

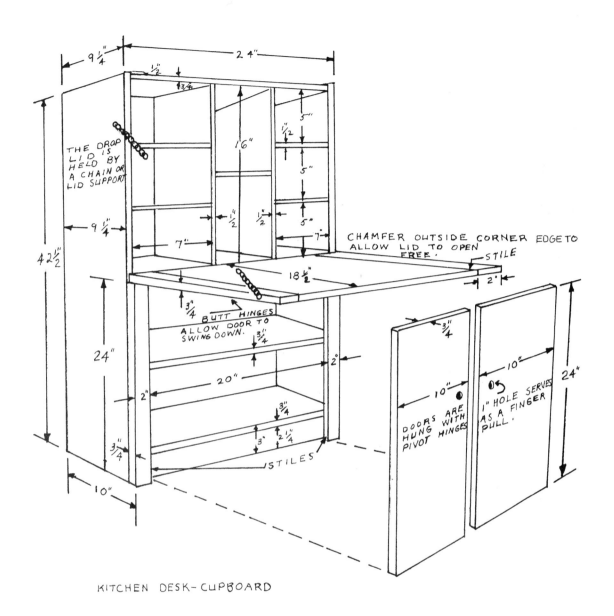

9¼"   24"
½"
¾"
5"
16"   1½"
5"

THE DROP
LID IS
HELD BY
A CHAIN OR
LID SUPPORT

9¼"   1½"   1½"   5"
7"   7"   CHAMFER OUTSIDE CORNER EDGE TO
ALLOW LID TO OPEN
FREE.   STILE

42½"   18½"   2"

¾"
BUTT HINGES
ALLOW DOOR TO
SWING DOWN.   ¾"

24"   2"

¾"   10"
20"

2"   10"   1" HOLE SERVES
AS A FINGER
PULL.   24"

DOORS ARE
HUNG WITH
PIVOT HINGES

¾"   ¾"
3"   2¼"

¾"
10"   STILES

KITCHEN DESK—CUPBOARD

KITCHEN
UTILITY CABINET.

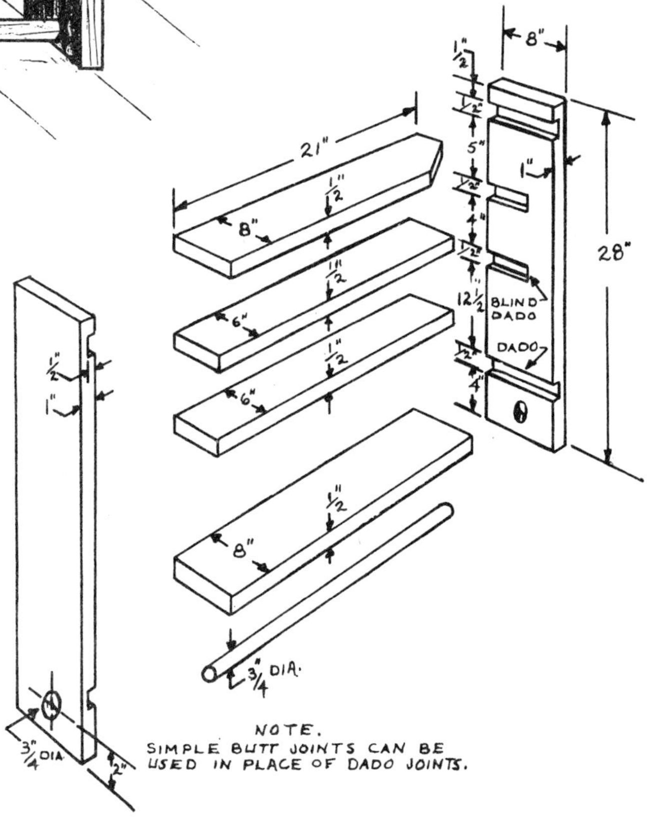

8"

1½"
1½"
5"

21"
1"
½"
8"

1"
½"

1"
½"
6"

28"

12½"

BLIND
DADO

DADO

6"
1"
½"

4"

8"
1"
½"

½"
1"

¾" DIA.

3"
¾ DIA

½"

NOTE.
SIMPLE BUTT JOINTS CAN BE
USED IN PLACE OF DADO JOINTS.

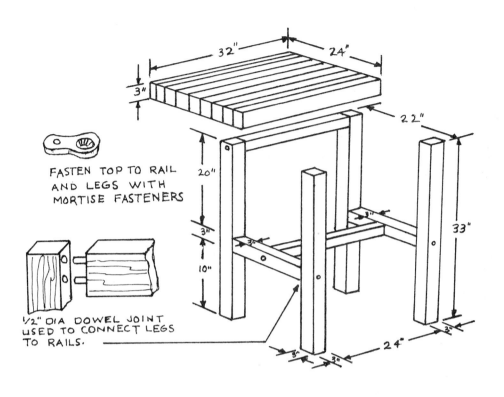

FASTEN TOP TO RAIL
AND LEGS WITH
MORTISE FASTENERS

1/2" DIA DOWEL JOINT
USED TO CONNECT LEGS
TO RAILS.

32" 24" 3" 22" 20" 3" 3" 33" 10" 3" 24" 3" 5" 3"

CHOPPING BLOCK

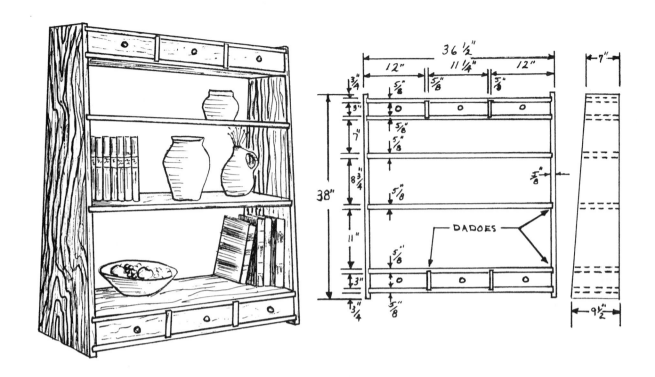

SLANTING WALL RACK

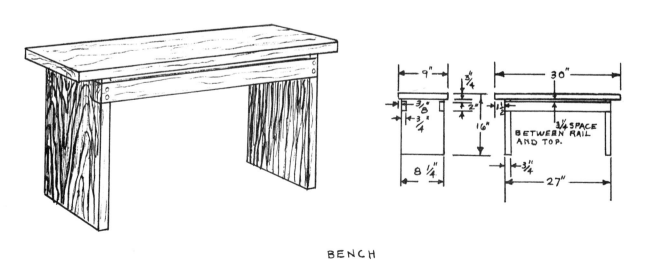

BENCH

SET OF STEPS

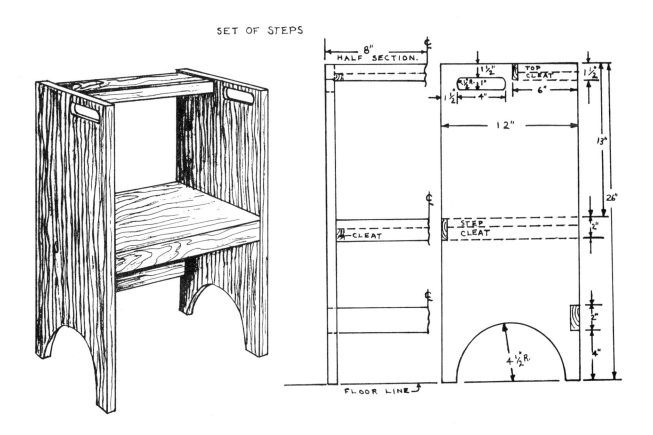

HALF SECTION.
8"
12"
1½"
TOP CLEAT
6"
1½"
1½"
4"
13"
26"
CLEAT
STEP CLEAT
2"
2"
4½" R.
2"
4"
FLOOR LINE

WALL CUPBOARD

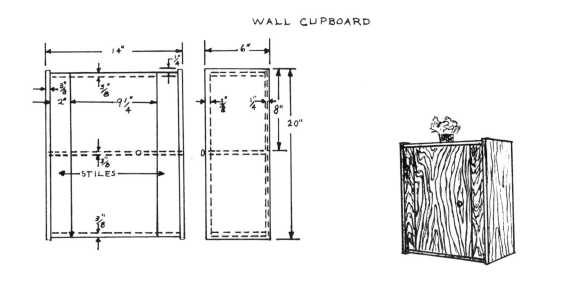

14"
6"
¼"
⅜"
2"
1⅝"
9¼"
⅜"
¼"
8"
20"
1⅜"
STILES
⅜"

BATH ROOM CATCH-ALL CABINET

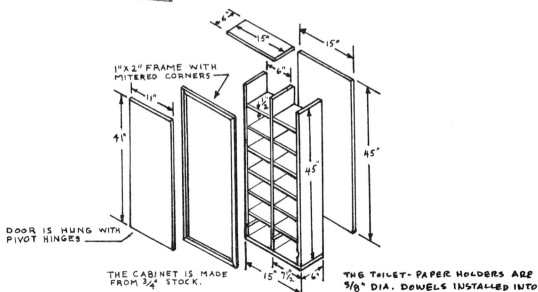

1" X 2" FRAME WITH MITERED CORNERS

DOOR IS HUNG WITH PIVOT HINGES

THE CABINET IS MADE FROM 3/4" STOCK.

THE TOILET-PAPER HOLDERS ARE 5/8" DIA. DOWELS INSTALLED INTO BLIND DADOES IN THE COMPARTMENTS LEFT OPEN.

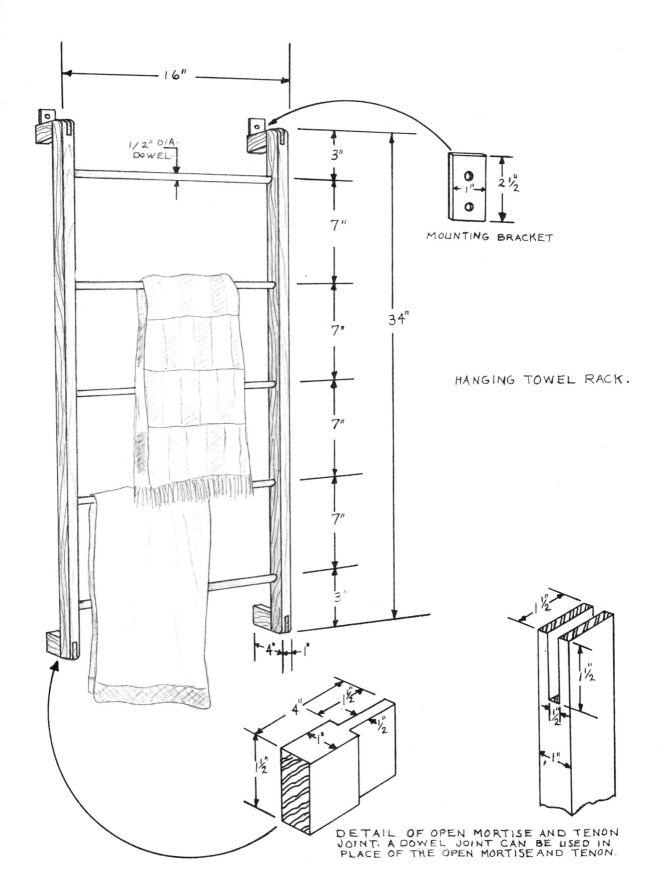

16"

1/2" DIA.
DOWEL·

MOUNTING BRACKET

2½"

1"

3"

7"

7"

7"

7"

7"

3"

34"

HANGING TOWEL RACK.

4"   1"

1½"

1½"

½"

1"

DETAIL OF OPEN MORTISE AND TENON
JOINT. A DOWEL JOINT CAN BE USED IN
PLACE OF THE OPEN MORTISE AND TENON.

4"   1½"

1"   ½"

1½"

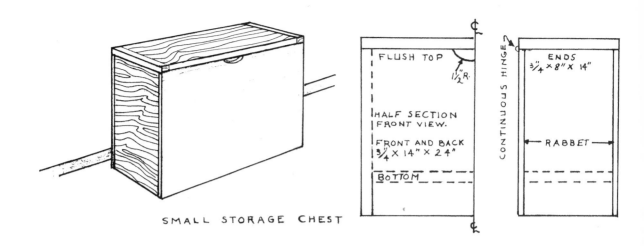

SMALL STORAGE CHEST

FLUSH TOP
1½"R.

HALF SECTION
FRONT VIEW.

FRONT AND BACK
¾" X 14" X 24"

BOTTOM

CONTINUOUS HINGE

ENDS
¾" X 8" X 14"

RABBET

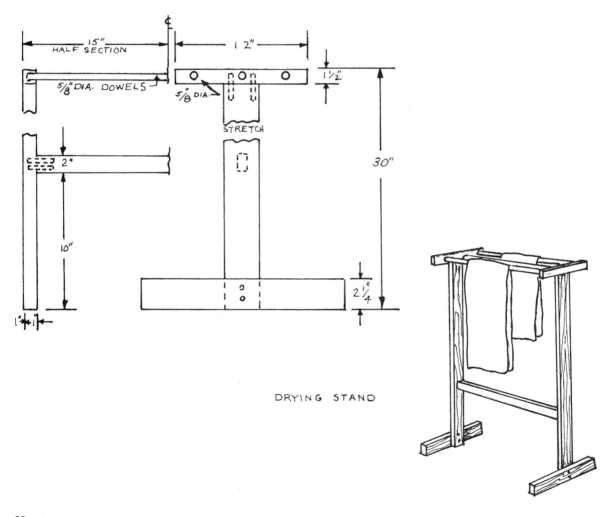

15"
HALF SECTION

12"

1½"

⅝" DIA. DOWELS

⅝" DIA.

STRETCH

2"

30"

10"

2¼"

1" 1"

DRYING STAND

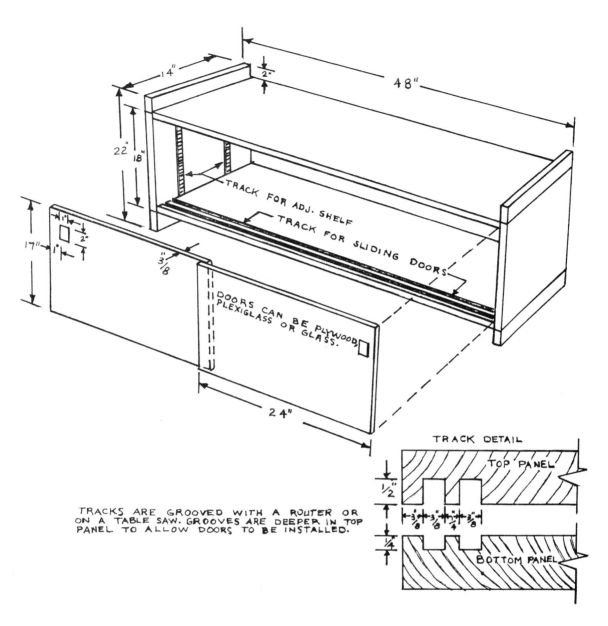

14"

48"

2"

22" 18"

TRACK FOR ADJ. SHELF

TRACK FOR SLIDING DOORS

17"

1"

2"

1"

3/8

DOORS CAN BE PLYWOOD, PLEXIGLASS OR GLASS.

24"

TRACK DETAIL

TOP PANEL

1/2"

3/8 3/8 1/4 3/8

1/4

BOTTOM PANEL

TRACKS ARE GROOVED WITH A ROUTER OR ON A TABLE SAW. GROOVES ARE DEEPER IN TOP PANEL TO ALLOW DOORS TO BE INSTALLED.

WALL CABINET

BAR/SERVER ON WHEELS

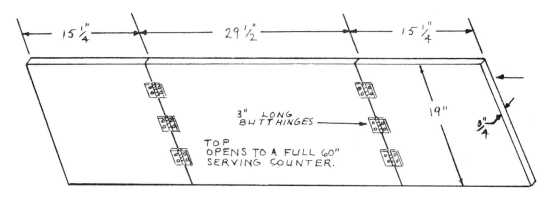

15 1/4"   29 1/2"   15 1/4"

3" LONG BUTT HINGES

19"

3/4"

TOP OPENS TO A FULL 60" SERVING COUNTER.

IF TOP IS MADE FROM WOOD USE SPAR VARNISH AS A PROTECTOR OF MOISTURE. TOP CAN ALSO BE COVERED WITH PLASTIC LAMINATE

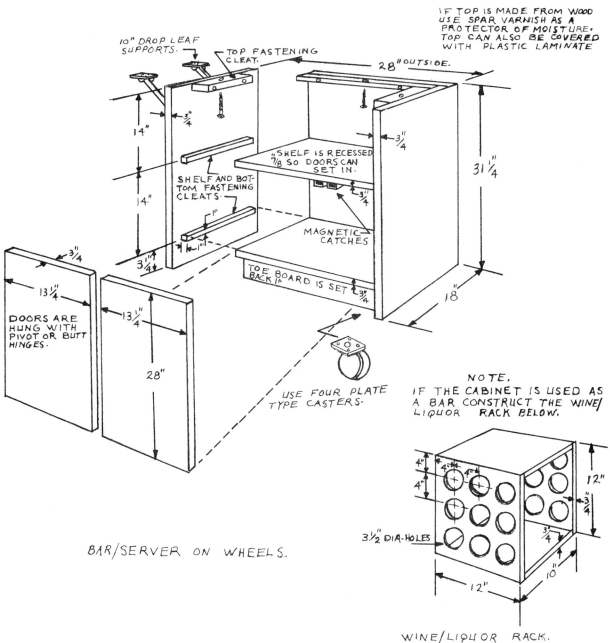

10" DROP LEAF SUPPORTS.

TOP FASTENING CLEAT.

28" OUTSIDE.

14"

3/4"

14"

SHELF AND BOTTOM FASTENING CLEATS.

SHELF IS RECESSED 7/8 SO DOORS CAN SET IN.

3/4"

31 1/4"

MAGNETIC CATCHES

1"

3 1/4"

1"

TOE BOARD IS SET BACK 1"

3/4"

18"

3/4"

13 1/4"

13 1/4"

DOORS ARE HUNG WITH PIVOT OR BUTT HINGES.

28"

USE FOUR PLATE TYPE CASTERS.

BAR/SERVER ON WHEELS.

NOTE.
IF THE CABINET IS USED AS A BAR CONSTRUCT THE WINE/ LIQUOR RACK BELOW.

4"   4"   4"

4"

12"

3/4"

3/4"

3 1/2" DIA. HOLES

12"

10"

WINE/LIQUOR RACK.

GUN CABINET

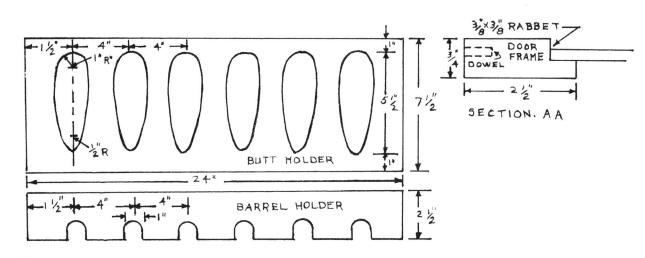

BUTT HOLDER

BARREL HOLDER

SECTION. AA

$\frac{3}{8}" \times \frac{3}{8}"$ RABBET
DOOR FRAME
DOWEL

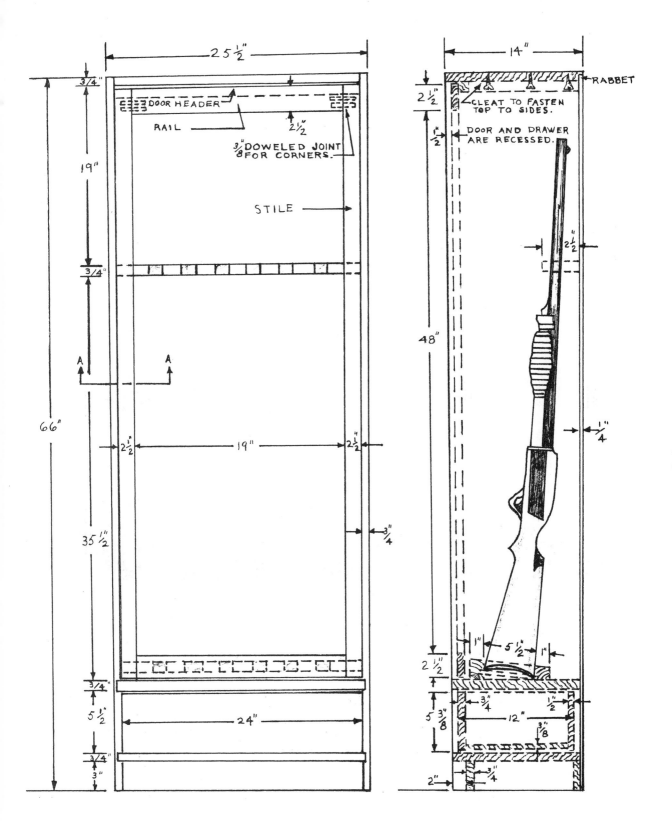

GUN CABINET

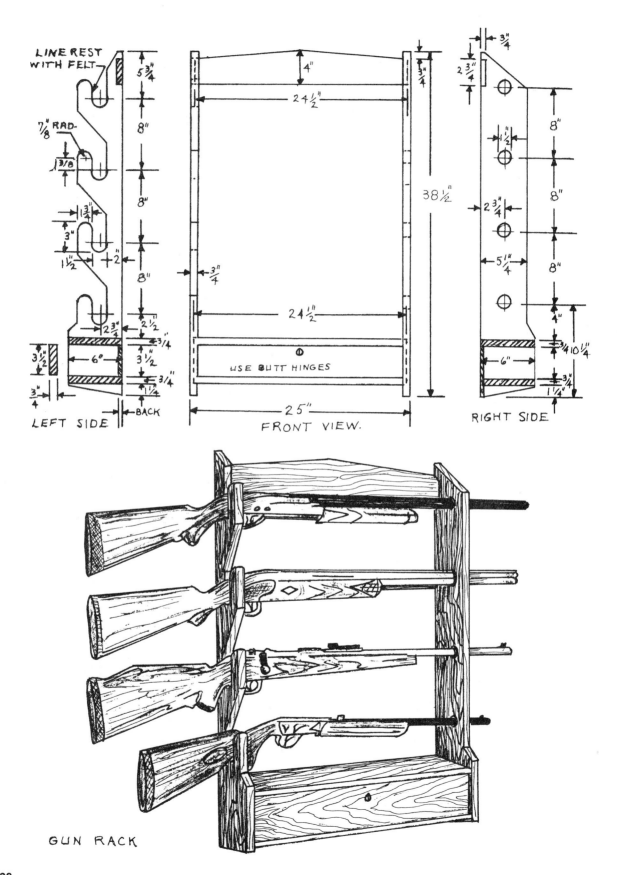

LINE REST WITH FELT

$\frac{7}{8}$" RAD.

$\frac{3}{8}$"

LEFT SIDE

BACK

FRONT VIEW.

USE BUTT HINGES

RIGHT SIDE

GUN RACK

COAT RACK SHOWN WITH
OPTIONAL CLOTHES HOOK

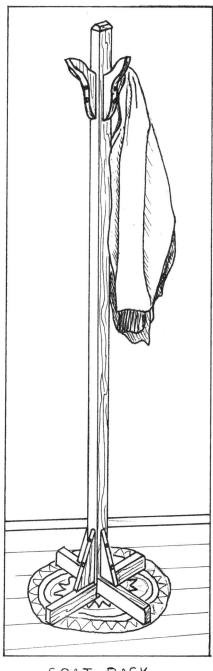

COAT RACK

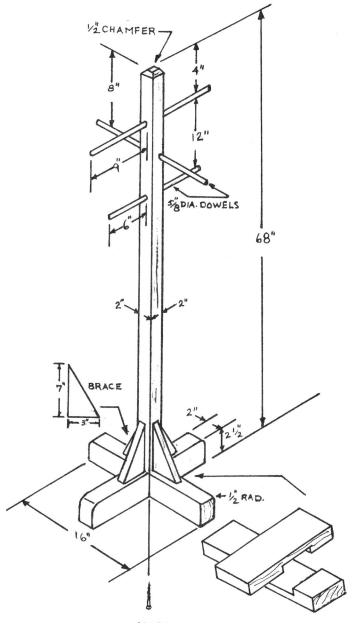

½" CHAMFER

4"

8"

12"

6"

5/8" DIA. DOWELS

68"

2"   2"

BRACE

7"

3"

2"

2½"

½" RAD.

16"

MIDDLE LAP JOINT USED
TO FASTEN BASE.

OPTIONAL
CLOTHES HOOK

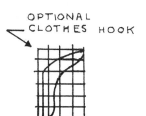

LOG BIN
WITH DRYING RACK.

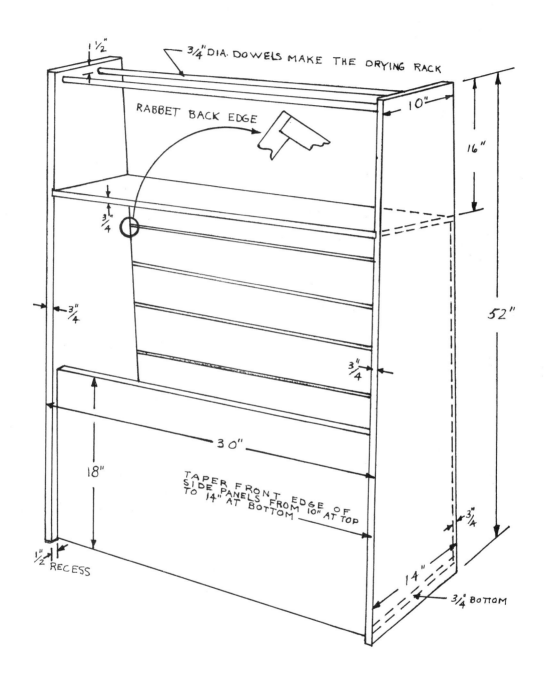

1½"

¾" DIA. DOWELS MAKE THE DRYING RACK

RABBET BACK EDGE

10"

16"

¾"

52"

¾"

¾"

30"

18"

TAPER FRONT EDGE OF
SIDE PANELS FROM 10" AT TOP
TO 14" AT BOTTOM

¾"

½" RECESS

14"

¾" BOTTOM

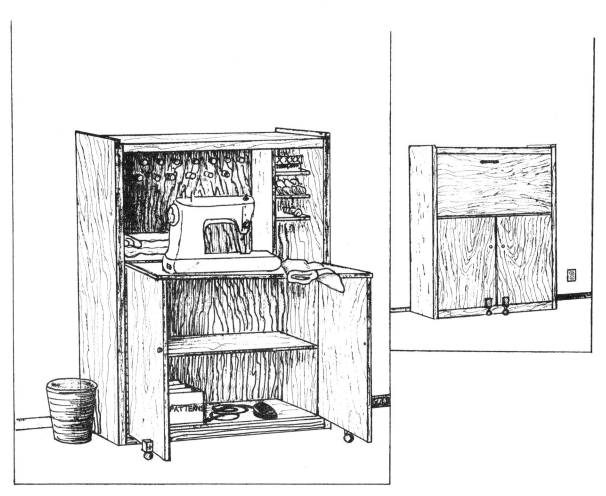

SEWING CENTER

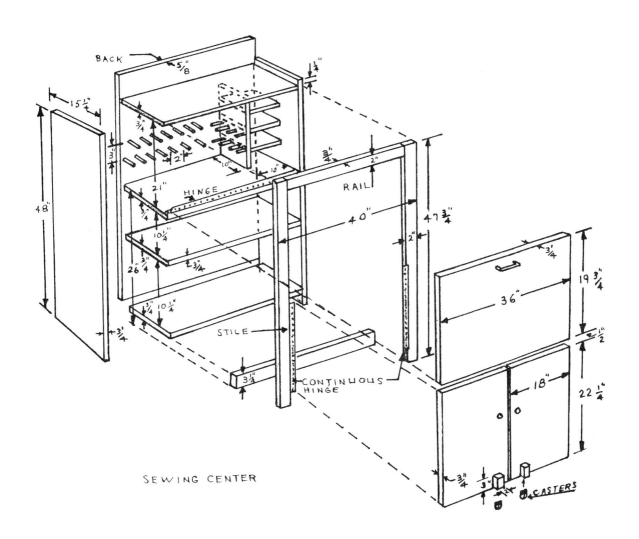

BACK

$\frac{5}{8}$"

$\frac{1}{4}$"

15$\frac{1}{4}$"

48"

$\frac{3}{4}$"

$\frac{3}{4}$"

3"

2"

10"

HINGE

10"

$\frac{3}{4}$"

RAIL

2"

$\frac{3}{4}$"

2"

47$\frac{3}{4}$"

21"

$\frac{3}{4}$"

40"

2"

10$\frac{1}{4}$"

$\frac{3}{4}$"

26$\frac{3}{4}$"

$\frac{3}{4}$"

10$\frac{1}{4}$"

STILE

$\frac{3}{4}$"

$\frac{3}{4}$"

CONTINUOUS
HINGE

$\frac{3}{4}$"

36"

19$\frac{3}{4}$"

$\frac{1}{2}$"

18"

22$\frac{1}{4}$"

$\frac{3}{4}$"

$\frac{3}{4}$"

CASTERS

SEWING CENTER

103

WOODWORKER'S BENCH

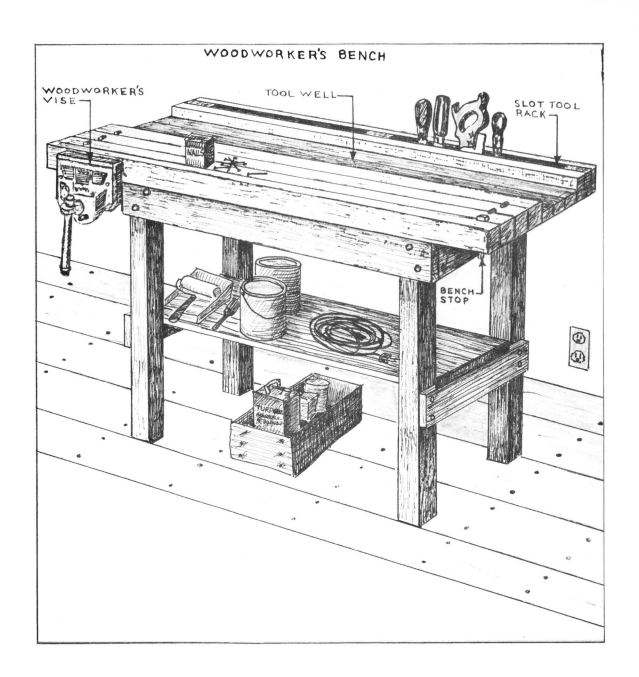

WOODWORKER'S VISE

TOOL WELL

SLOT TOOL RACK

BENCH STOP

NAILS

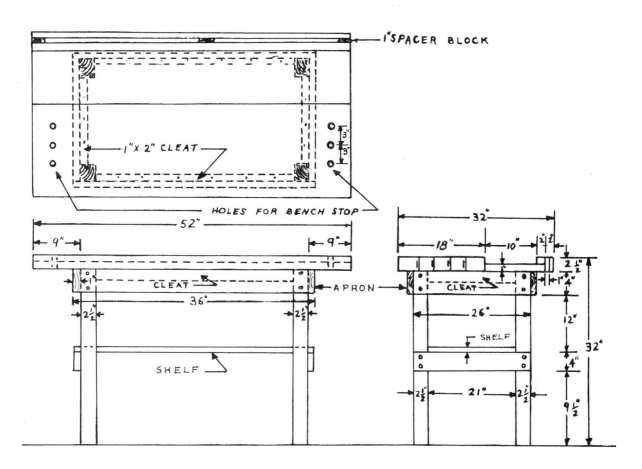

1" SPACER BLOCK

1" x 2" CLEAT

3"
3"

HOLES FOR BENCH STOP

52"

9"   9"

CLEAT   APRON

36"

2 1/2"   2 1/2"

SHELF

32"

18"   10"   2 1/2"

2 1/2"

CLEAT

1"
4"

26"

12"

SHELF

4"

2 1/2"   21"   2 1/2"

9 1/2"

32"

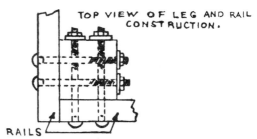

TOP VIEW OF LEG AND RAIL
CONSTRUCTION.

RAILS

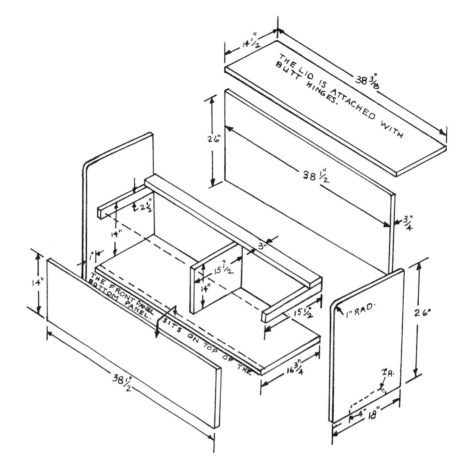

$14\frac{1}{2}$"

THE LID IS ATTACHED WITH BUTT HINGES.

$38\frac{3}{8}$"

26"

$38\frac{1}{2}$"

$\frac{3}{4}$"

$2\frac{1}{2}$"

14"

3"

$15\frac{1}{2}$"

14"

1"

$15\frac{1}{2}$"

THE FRONT PANEL SITS ON TOP OF THE BOTTOM PANEL.

14"

$16\frac{3}{4}$"

$38\frac{1}{2}$"

1" RAD.

26"

2" R.

R-4" 18"

STORAGE BENCH / TOY CHEST

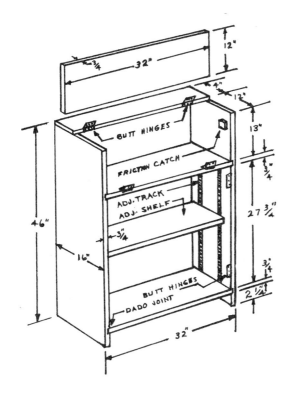

BUTT HINGES

FRICTION CATCH

ADJ. TRACK
ADJ. SHELF

BUTT HINGES
DADO JOINT

12"

¾"

32"

4"

12"

13"

¾"

27¾"

¾"

46"

16"

¾"

2¼"

32"

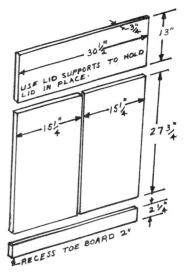

3"

30½"

13"

USE LID SUPPORTS TO HOLD
LID IN PLACE.

15¼"

15¼"

15¼"

27¾"

2¼"

RECESS TOE BOARD 2"

HOME BAR

TV CONSOLE
HOLDS UP TO A 21" PORTABLE TV

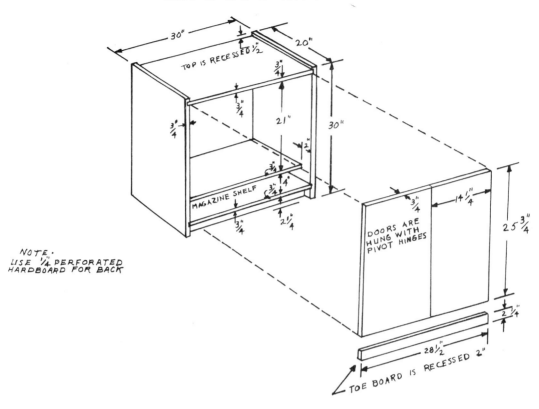

30"

20"

TOP IS RECESSED 1/2"

3/4"

3/4"

3/4"

21"

30"

2"

MAGAZINE SHELF

3/4"

4"

3/4"

3/4"

2 1/4"

3/4"

14 1/4"

DOORS ARE HUNG WITH PIVOT HINGES

25 3/4"

2 1/4"

28 1/2"

TOE BOARD IS RECESSED 2"

NOTE:
USE 1/4" PERFORATED
HARDBOARD FOR BACK

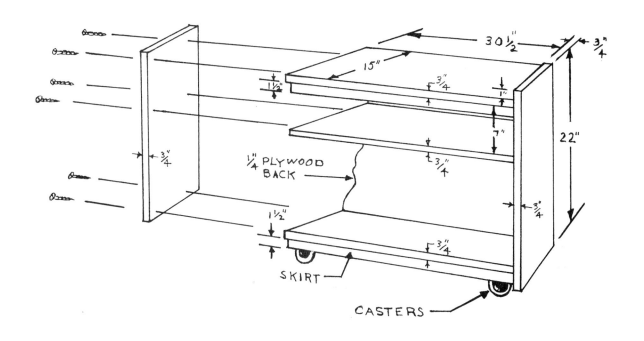

30½"

3"/4

15"

1½"

3"/4

1"

3"/4

22"

7"

¼" PLYWOOD BACK

3"/4

3"/4

3"/4

1½"

3"/4

SKIRT

CASTERS

PORTABLE TV STAND

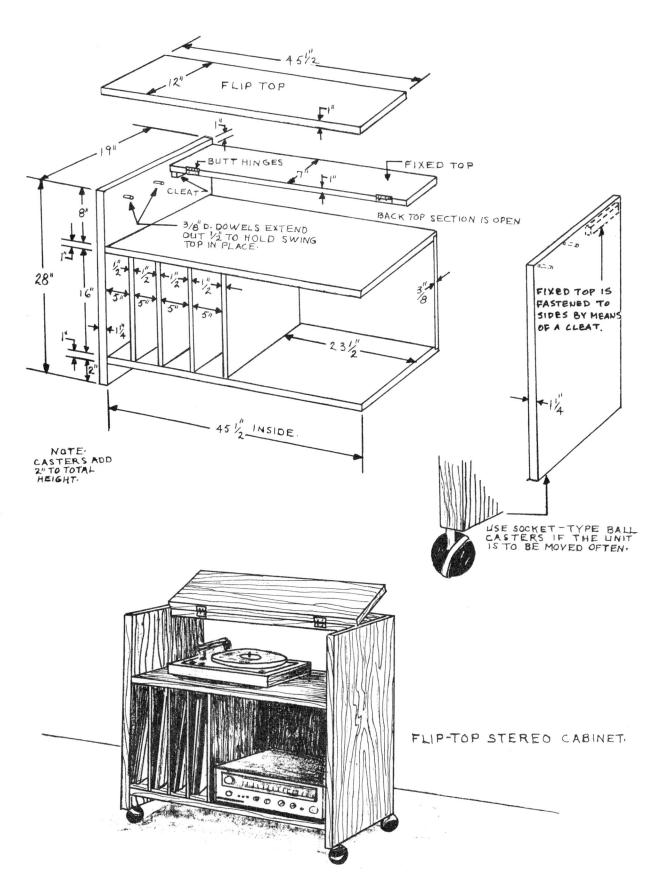

45½"

12"   FLIP TOP

1"

19"   1"

BUTT HINGES   2" 1"   FIXED TOP

CLEAT

8"   3/8" D. DOWELS EXTEND   BACK TOP SECTION IS OPEN
OUT ½" TO HOLD SWING
1"   TOP IN PLACE.

28"   ½" ½" ½" ½"   3"/8

16"   5" 5" 5" 5"   FIXED TOP IS
FASTENED TO
SIDES BY MEANS
OF A CLEAT.

1"   1¼"   23½"

2"

45½" INSIDE.   1¼"

NOTE:
CASTERS ADD
2" TO TOTAL
HEIGHT.

USE SOCKET-TYPE BALL
CASTERS IF THE UNIT
IS TO BE MOVED OFTEN.

FLIP-TOP STEREO CABINET.

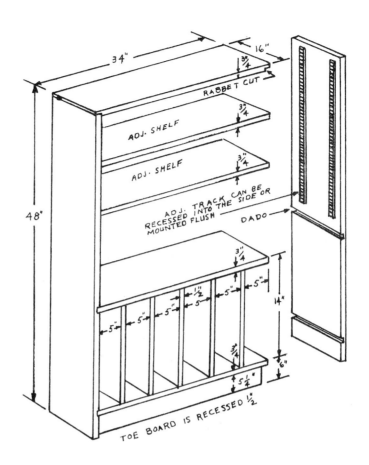

34"
16"
3/4"
RABBET CUT
3/4"
ADJ. SHELF
3/4"
ADJ. SHELF
48"
ADJ. TRACK CAN BE
RECESSED INTO THE SIDE OR
MOUNTED FLUSH
DADO
3/4"
1/2" 5" 5"
5" 5" 5"
14"
5" 5" 5"
3/4"
6"
5 1/4"
TOE BOARD IS RECESSED 1 1/2"

VERTICAL STEREO CENTER.

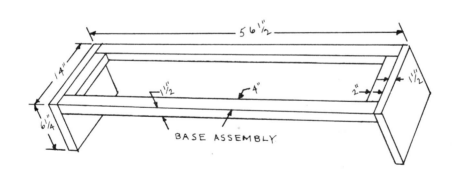

BASE ASSEMBLY

56 1/2"

14"

6 1/4"

1 1/2"

4"

2"

1 1/2"

STEREO CENTER
WITH BAR.

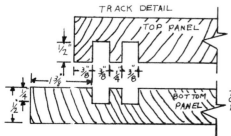

TRACK DETAIL

TOP PANEL

BOTTOM PANEL

1/2"

1 3/8"

3/8"

3/8"

1/4"

3/8"

1/4"

1/2"

TRACKS ARE GROOVED WITH A ROUTER OR
ON A TABLE SAW. GROOVES ARE DEEPER IN TOP
PANEL TO ALLOW DOORS TO BE INSTALLED.

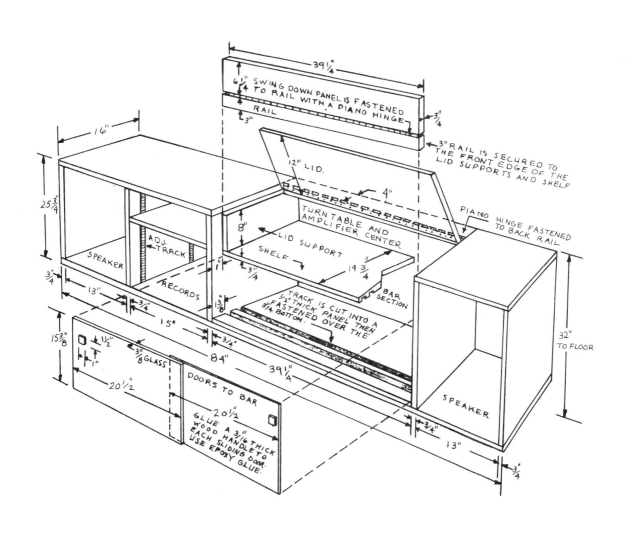

39¼"

6¼" SWING DOWN PANEL IS FASTENED
TO RAIL WITH A PIANO HINGE

RAIL

3"

¾"

3" RAIL IS SECURED TO
THE FRONT EDGE OF THE
LID SUPPORTS AND SHELF

12" LID.

4"

PIANO HINGE FASTENED
TO BACK RAIL

16"

25¾"

TURN TABLE AND
AMPLIFIER CENTER

8"

LID SUPPORT

ADJ.
TRACK

SPEAKER

RECORDS

SHELF

14 ¾"

¾"

3"

BAR
SECTION

¾"

13"

¾"

1¾"

TRACK IS CUT INTO A
½" THICK PANEL THEN
FASTENED OVER THE
¾" BOTTOM.

32"
TO FLOOR

SPEAKER

15"

¾"

84"

39¼"

15⅜"

1½"

1"

3/16 GLASS

20½"

DOORS TO BAR

20½"

GLUE A 3/16" THICK
WOOD HANDLE TO
EACH SLIDING DOOR.
USE EPOXY GLUE.

13"

¾"

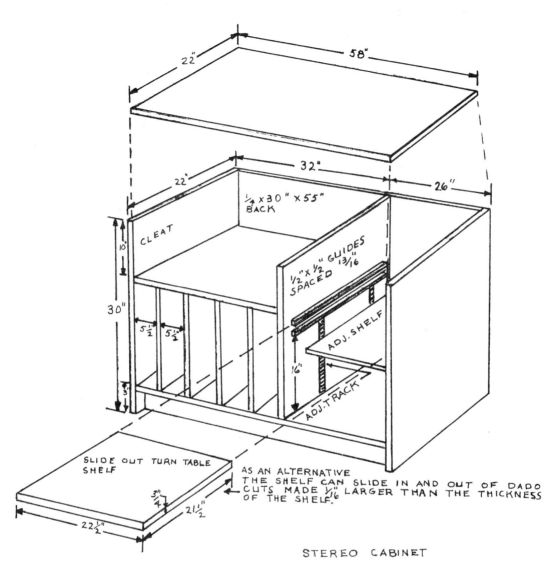

22"

58"

22"

32"

26"

¼ x 30" x 55"
BACK

CLEAT

10"

½" x ½" GUIDES
SPACED 13/16

30"

5½" 5½"

ADJ. SHELF

16"

3"

ADJ. TRACK

SLIDE OUT TURN TABLE
SHELF

AS AN ALTERNATIVE
THE SHELF CAN SLIDE IN AND OUT OF DADO
CUTS MADE 1/16" LARGER THAN THE THICKNESS
OF THE SHELF.

3"
4

21½"

22½"

STEREO CABINET

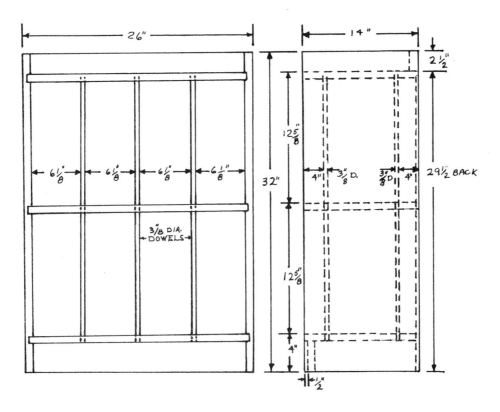

26"

6 1/8" 6 1/8" 6 1/8" 6 1/8"

3/8" DIA.
DOWELS

32"

14"

2 1/2"

12 5/8"

4"   3/8" D.   3/8" D   4"   29 1/2" BACK

12 5/8"

4"

1/2"

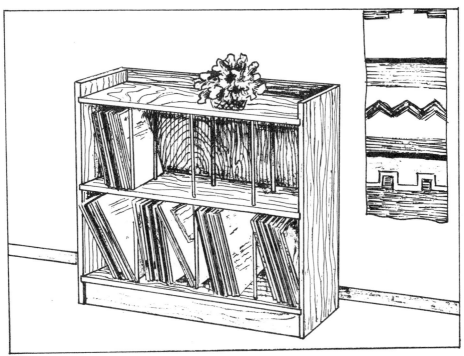

RECORD CABINET

115

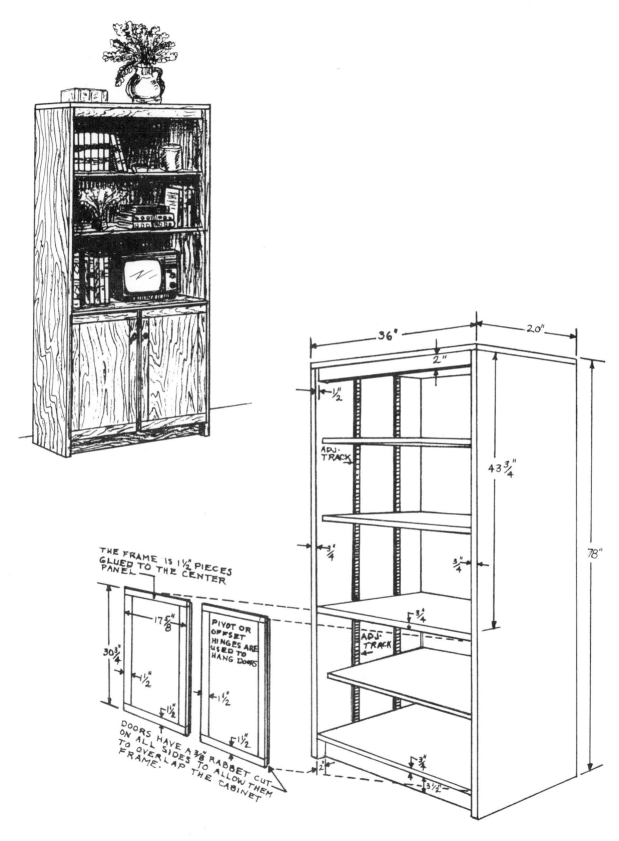

THE FRAME IS 1½" PIECES
GLUED TO THE CENTER
PANEL

17⅝"

30¾"

1½"

1½"

PIVOT OR
OFFSET
HINGES ARE
USED TO
HANG DOORS

1½"

1½"

DOORS HAVE A ⅜" RABBET CUT
ON ALL SIDES TO ALLOW THEM
TO OVERLAP THE CABINET
FRAME.

36"

20"

2"

½"

ADJ.
TRACK

43¾"

¾"

¾"

78"

¾"

ADJ.
TRACK

2"

¾"

3½"

UPRIGHT WALL CABINET.

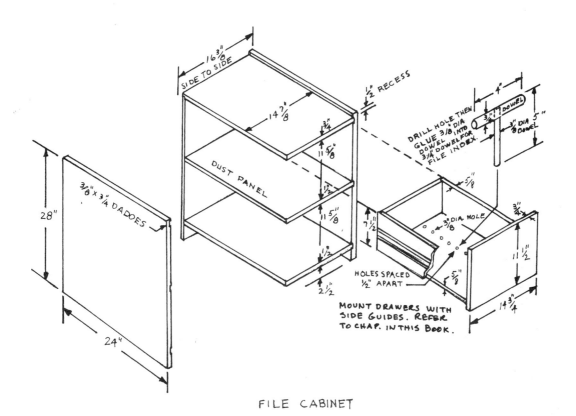

16 3/8" SIDE TO SIDE

1/2" RECESS

14 7/8"

3/4"

5/8"

DUST PANEL

1/2"

11 5/8"

1/2"

28"

3/8" X 3/4 DADOES

2 1/2"

24"

DRILL HOLE THEN GLUE 3/8 DIA. DOWEL INTO 3/4 DOWEL FOR FILE INDEX.

4"

DOWEL

3/4"

5"

3/8" DIA 3/4 DOWEL

5/8"

3/8" DIA. HOLE

3/4"

7 1/2"

11 1/2"

5/8"

HOLES SPACED 1/2" APART

14 3/4"

MOUNT DRAWERS WITH SIDE GUIDES. REFER TO CHAP. IN THIS BOOK.

FILE CABINET

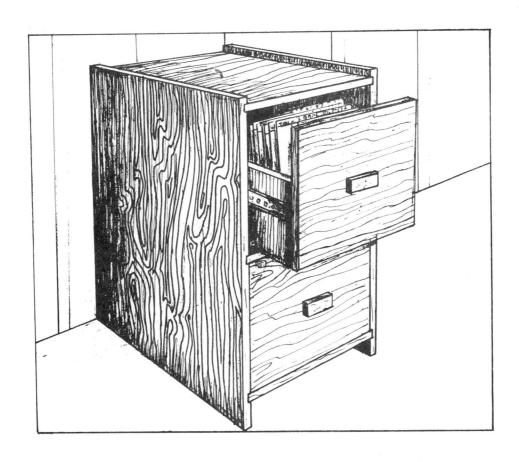

WALL CABINET WITH MANY USES.
USE AS A BAR, A STEREO CENTER, BOOKS, ETC.

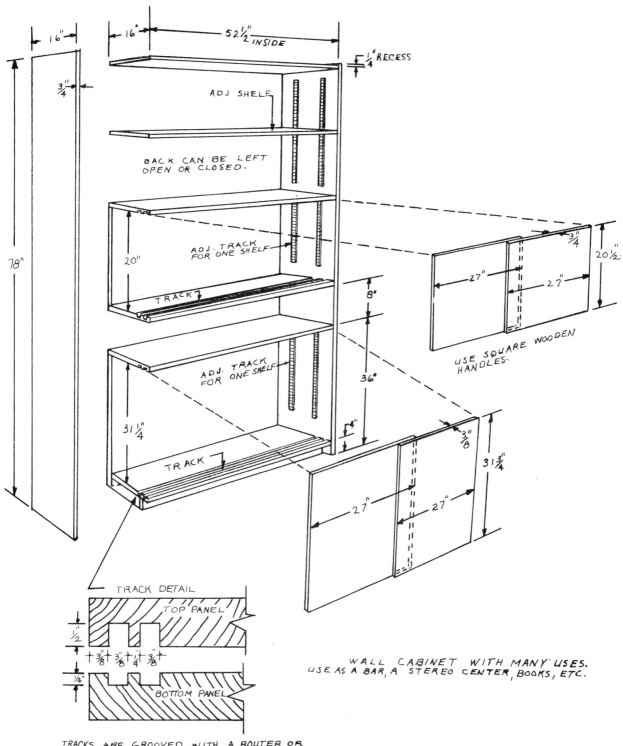

16"

16"

52½" INSIDE

¼" RECESS

¾"

ADJ SHELF

BACK CAN BE LEFT
OPEN OR CLOSED.

78"

ADJ. TRACK
FOR ONE SHELF

20"

TRACK

8"

36"

ADJ. TRACK
FOR ONE SHELF

31¼"

4"

TRACK

¾"

20½"

27"

27"

USE SQUARE WOODEN
HANDLES.

⅜"

31¾"

27"

27"

TRACK DETAIL

TOP PANEL

½"

⅜" ⅜" ¼" ⅜"

¼"

BOTTOM PANEL

TRACKS ARE GROOVED WITH A ROUTER OR
ON A TABLE SAW. GROOVES ARE DEEPER IN TOP
PANEL TO ALLOW DOORS TO BE INSTALLED.

WALL CABINET WITH MANY USES.
USE AS A BAR, A STEREO CENTER, BOOKS, ETC.

OPEN ROOM DIVIDER

SHOWN ARE TWO DIVIDERS SIDE BY SIDE.

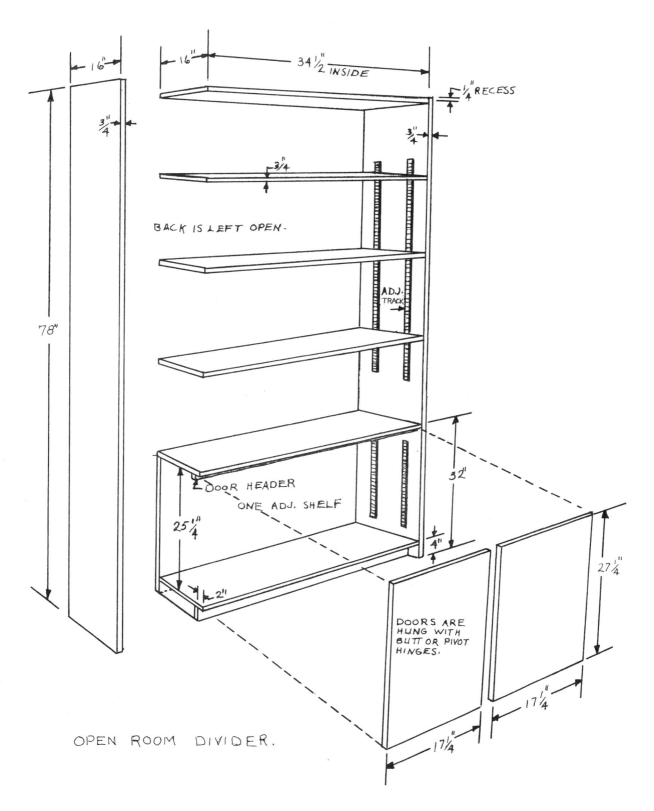

16"

16"

34 1/2" INSIDE

1/4" RECESS

3/4

3/4

3/4

BACK IS LEFT OPEN.

78"

ADJ. TRACK

DOOR HEADER

ONE ADJ. SHELF

32"

25 1/4"

4"

27 1/4"

DOORS ARE HUNG WITH BUTT OR PIVOT HINGES.

2"

17 1/4"

17 1/4"

OPEN ROOM DIVIDER.

NOTE: THIS CABINET CAN ALSO BE PLACED AGAINST A WALL.

KNEE-HOLE DESK.

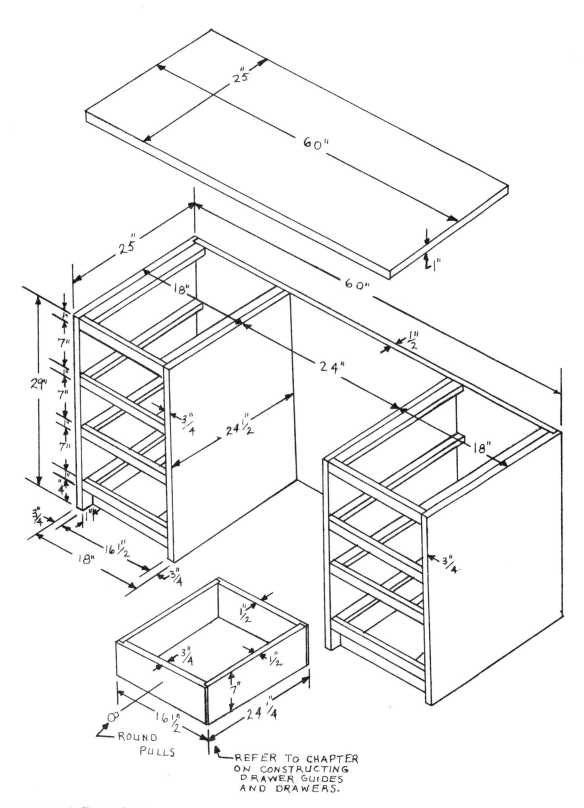

25"

60"

1"

25"

60"

18"

1"
7"
7"
1"
7"
1"
29"

1½"

24"

3/4"

24½"

18"

3/4"

3/4"
1"
18"
16½"
3/4"

1½"

½"

3/4"

7"

16½"

24¼"

O

ROUND
PULLS

REFER TO CHAPTER
ON CONSTRUCTING
DRAWER GUIDES
AND DRAWERS.

KNEE-HOLE DESK.

SLANT TOP DESK

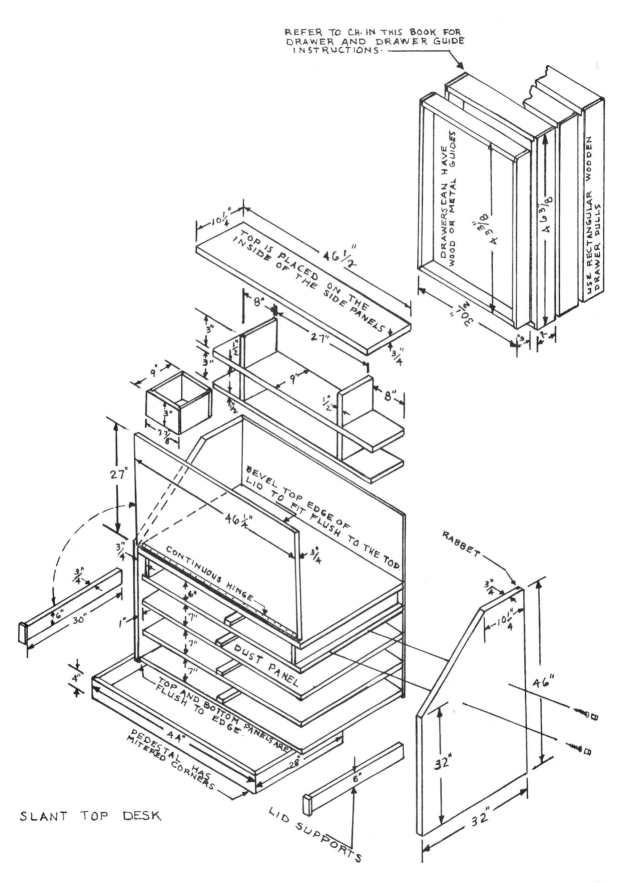

REFER TO CH. IN THIS BOOK FOR
DRAWER AND DRAWER GUIDE
INSTRUCTIONS.

DRAWERS CAN HAVE
WOOD OR METAL GUIDES

USE RECTANGULAR WOODEN
DRAWER PULLS

TOP IS PLACED ON THE
INSIDE OF THE SIDE PANELS

BEVEL TOP EDGE OF
LID TO FIT FLUSH TO THE TOP

RABBET

CONTINUOUS HINGE

DUST PANEL

TOP AND BOTTOM PANELS ARE
FLUSH TO EDGE

PEDESTAL HAS
MITERED CORNERS

SLANT TOP DESK

LID SUPPORTS

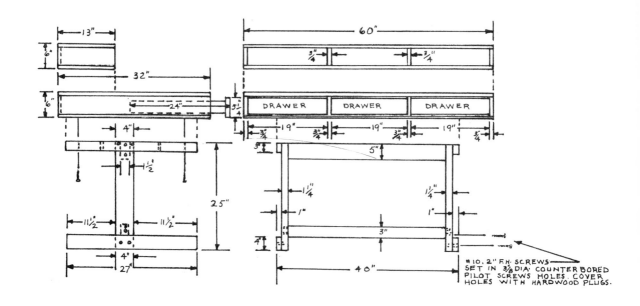

13"
6"
32"
6"
24"
5 1/4"
4"
1 1/2"
25"
11 1/2"
11 1/2"
4"
27"

60"
3/4"
3/4"

DRAWER   DRAWER   DRAWER

3/4"
19"   3/4"   19"   3/4"   19"   3/4"
3 1/2"
5"
1 1/4"   1 1/4"
1"   1"
3"
4"
40"

#10, 2" F.H. SCREWS
SET IN 3/8 DIA. COUNTER BORED
PILOT SCREWS HOLES. COVER
HOLES WITH HARDWOOD PLUGS.

HOME DESK

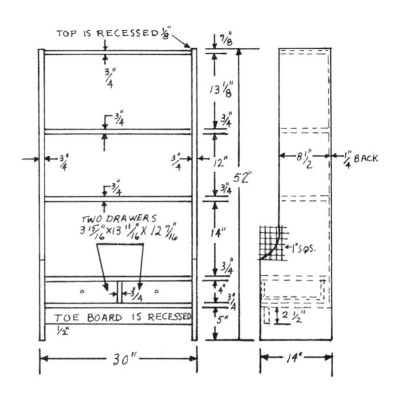

TOP IS RECESSED ⅛"

$\frac{7}{8}$"

$\frac{3}{4}$"

13 ⅛"

$\frac{3}{4}$"

$\frac{3}{4}$"

$\frac{3}{4}$"

12"

$\frac{3}{4}$"

52"

8 ½"

¼" BACK

$\frac{3}{4}$"

TWO DRAWERS
3 $\frac{15}{16}$" X 13 $\frac{11}{16}$" X 12 $\frac{7}{16}$"

14"

1" SQS.

$\frac{3}{4}$"

$\frac{3}{4}$"

4"

$\frac{3}{4}$"

TOE BOARD IS RECESSED
½"

5"

2 ½"

30"

14"

BOOKCASE WITH DRAWERS

127

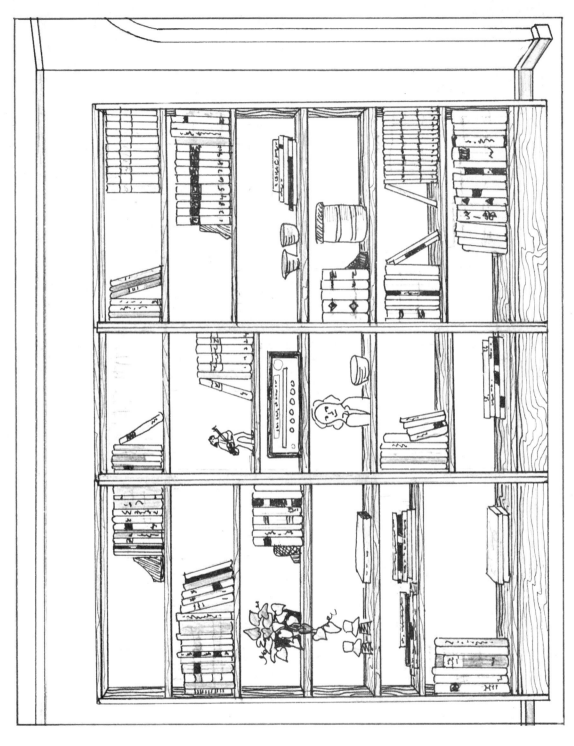

MODULAR OPEN WALL SHELVING.

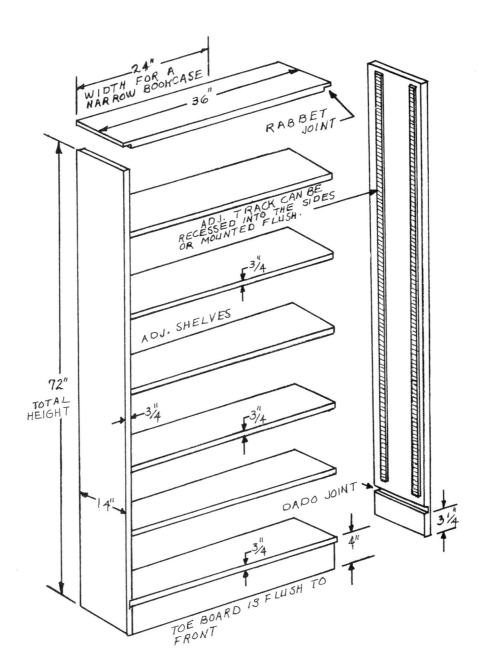

24"
WIDTH FOR A
NARROW BOOKCASE

36"

RABBET JOINT

ADJ. TRACK CAN BE
RECESSED INTO THE SIDES
OR MOUNTED FLUSH.

$3/4"$

ADJ. SHELVES

72"
TOTAL
HEIGHT

$3/4"$

$3/4"$

14"

DADO JOINT

$3^{1/4"}$

$3/4"$

4"

TOE BOARD IS FLUSH TO
FRONT

MODULAR
OPEN WALL SHELVING

BOOK/MAGAZINE CABINET

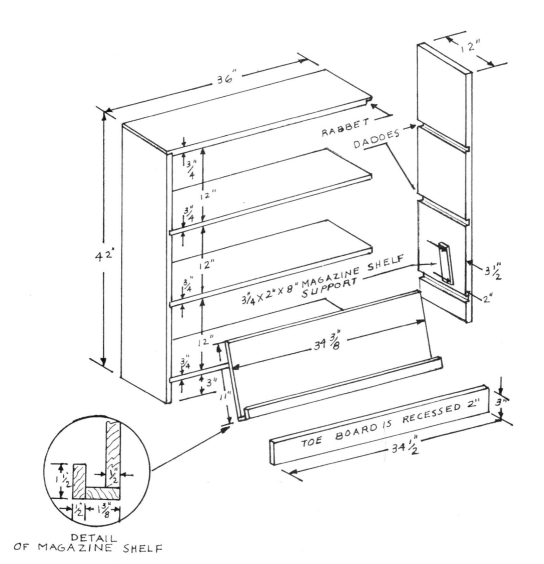

36"

RABBET

DADOES

12"

3"/4

12"

3"/4

42"

12"

3"/4

3/4" X 2" X 8" MAGAZINE SHELF
SUPPORT

12"

3"/4

3"

11"

3 1/2"

2"

34 3/8"

3"

TOE BOARD IS RECESSED 2"

34 1/2"

1 1/2"

1/2"

1/2"

1 3/8"

DETAIL
OF MAGAZINE SHELF

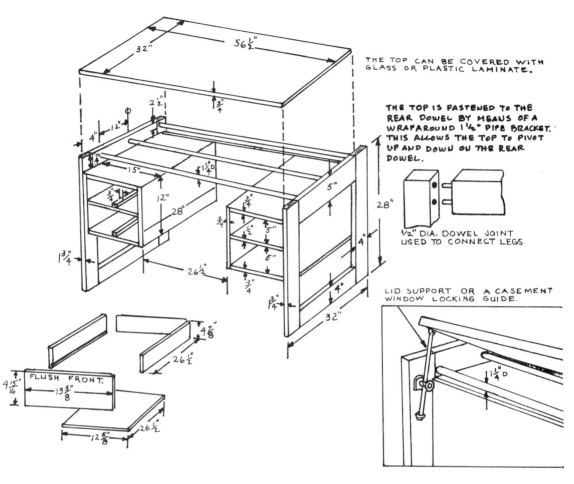

THE TOP CAN BE COVERED WITH
GLASS OR PLASTIC LAMINATE.

THE TOP IS FASTENED TO THE
REAR DOWEL BY MEANS OF A
WRAPAROUND $1\frac{1}{4}$" PIPE BRACKET.
THIS ALLOWS THE TOP TO PIVOT
UP AND DOWN ON THE REAR
DOWEL.

$\frac{1}{2}$" DIA. DOWEL JOINT
USED TO CONNECT LEGS

LID SUPPORT OR A CASEMENT
WINDOW LOCKING GUIDE.

FLUSH FRONT.

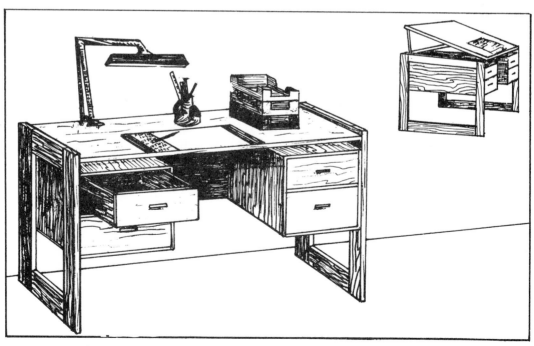

ADJUSTABLE TOP DESK.

THE MASTER BEDROOM

THESE MODERN FURNITURE PROJECTS ARE FOUND ON THE FOLLOWING PAGES.

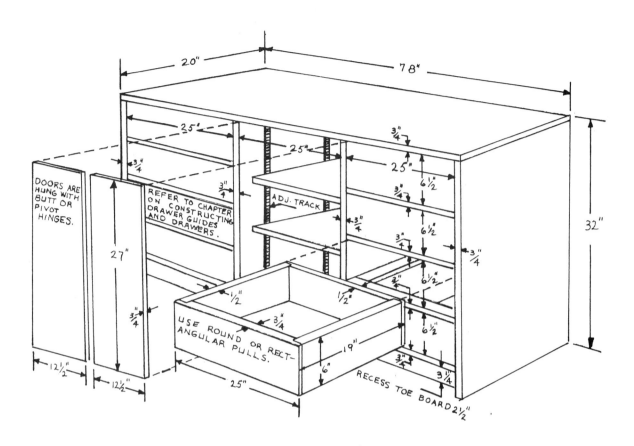

20"
78"
25'
25"
3/4"
25"
6 1/2"
3/4
3/4"
32"
3/4"
DOORS ARE
HUNG WITH
BUTT OR
PIVOT
HINGES.
3/4
3"
4
REFER TO CHAPTER
ON CONSTRUCTING
DRAWER GUIDES
AND DRAWERS.
ADJ. TRACK
6 1/2"
3/4
27"
3/4
3/4"
6 1/2"
3/4
1/2"
1/2"
3/4
USE ROUND OR RECT-
ANGULAR PULLS.
3/4
6 1/2"
12 1/2"
12 1/2"
19"
6"
25"
3/4
3/4
RECESS TOE BOARD 2 1/2"

TRIPLE DRESSER

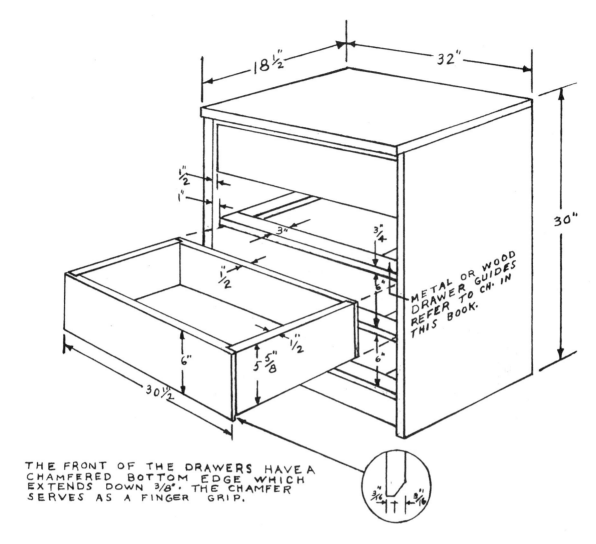

18½" 32"

30"

½"
1"
3"
¾"
6"
6"

½"
½"

6"
5⅝"
30½"

METAL OR WOOD
DRAWER GUIDES
REFER TO CH. IN
THIS BOOK.

THE FRONT OF THE DRAWERS HAVE A
CHAMFERED BOTTOM EDGE WHICH
EXTENDS DOWN 3/8". THE CHAMFER
SERVES AS A FINGER GRIP.

3/16" 3/16"

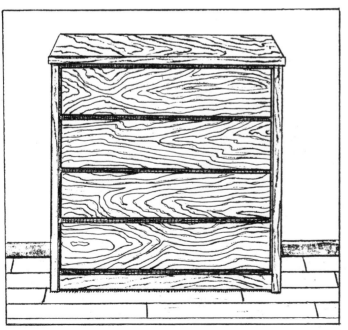

FOUR DRAWER
BACHELOR CHEST.

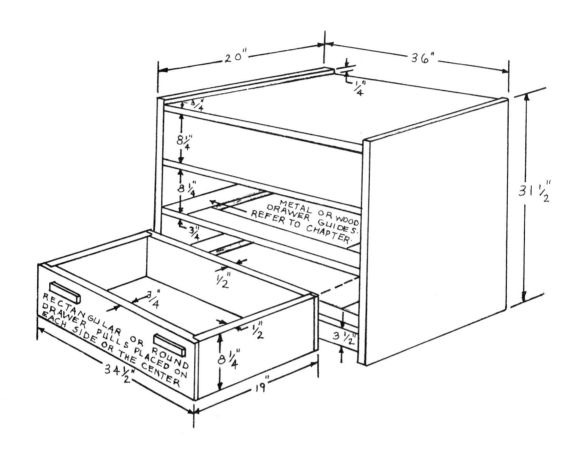

20"
36"
1/4"
3/4"
8 1/4"
8 1/4"
3/4"
METAL OR WOOD
DRAWER GUIDES.
REFER TO CHAPTER.
1/2"
31 1/2"
3/4"
1/2"
RECTANGULAR OR ROUND
DRAWER PULLS PLACED ON
EACH SIDE OR THE CENTER
8 1/4"
3 1/2"
34 1/2"
19"

CHEST OF THREE DRAWERS

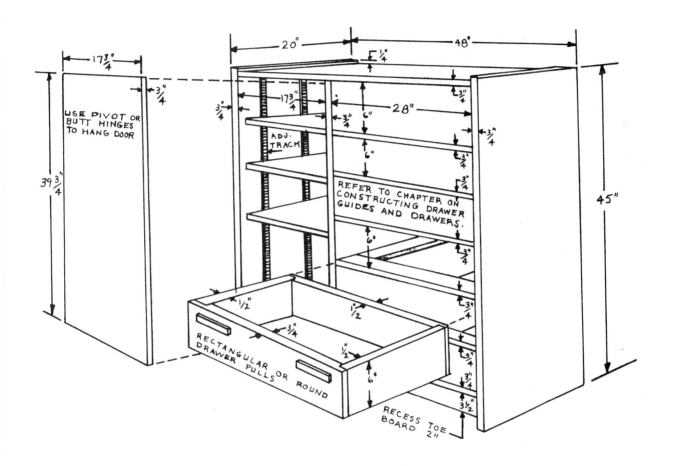

17¾"

3/4"

USE PIVOT OR
BUTT HINGES
TO HANG DOOR

39¾"

20"

¼"

17¾"

3/4"

3/4"

ADJ.
TRACK

48"

3/4"

28"

3/4"

6"

3/4"

6"

3/4"

REFER TO CHAPTER ON
CONSTRUCTING DRAWER
GUIDES AND DRAWERS.

6"

3/4"

45"

3/4"

½"

½"

3/4"

½"

RECTANGULAR OR ROUND
DRAWER PULLS

6"

3/4"

3/4"

3/4"

3½"

RECESS TOE
BOARD 2"

SIX DRAWER WARDROBE.

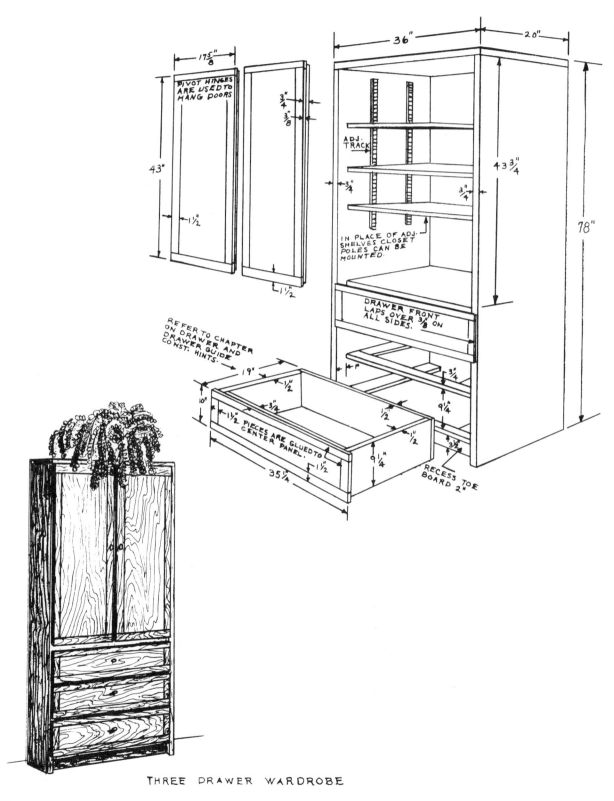

THREE DRAWER WARDROBE

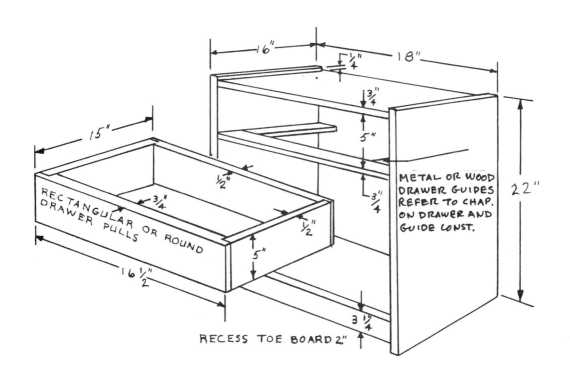

16"
1/4"
18"
3/4"
5"
15"
22"
1/2"
3/4"
RECTANGULAR OR ROUND
DRAWER PULLS
3/4
1/2"
5"
METAL OR WOOD
DRAWER GUIDES
REFER TO CHAP.
ON DRAWER AND
GUIDE CONST.
16 1/2"
3 1/4"
RECESS TOE BOARD 2"

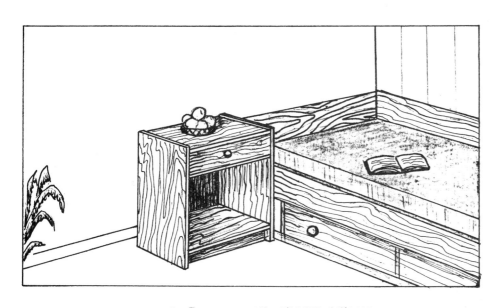

ONE DRAWER NIGHT STAND

SIX DRAWER WARDROBE

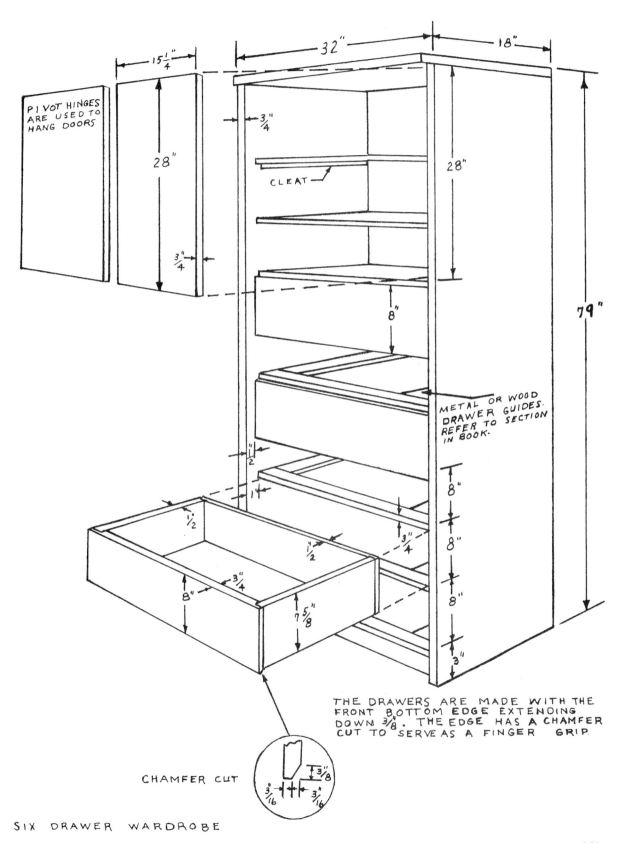

PIVOT HINGES
ARE USED TO
HANG DOORS

15 1/4"

28"

3/4"

32"

18"

3/4"

CLEAT

28"

8"

79"

METAL OR WOOD
DRAWER GUIDES.
REFER TO SECTION
IN BOOK.

1 1/2"

1"

1/2"

1/2"

3/4"

8"

8"

8"

8"

3/4"

3"

7 5/8"

THE DRAWERS ARE MADE WITH THE
FRONT BOTTOM EDGE EXTENDING
DOWN 3/8". THE EDGE HAS A CHAMFER
CUT TO SERVE AS A FINGER GRIP.

CHAMFER CUT

3/8"

3/16"

3/16"

SIX DRAWER WARDROBE

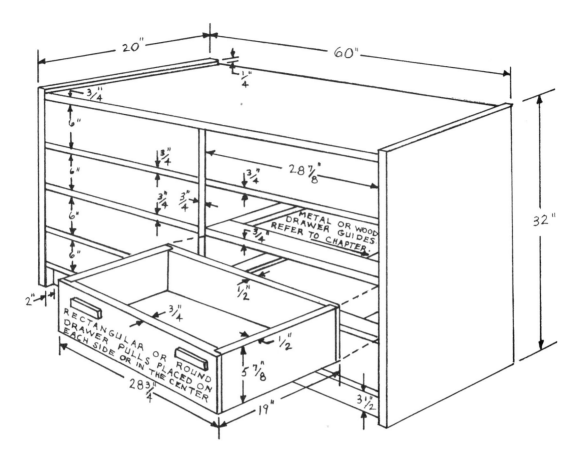

20"

60"

¼"

¾"

6"

¾"

6"

28⅞"

¾"

¾"

¾"

6"

32"

METAL OR WOOD
DRAWER GUIDES.
REFER TO CHAPTER.

¾"

6"

½"

2"

¾"

RECTANGULAR OR ROUND
DRAWER PULLS PLACED ON
EACH SIDE OR IN THE CENTER

½"

5⅞"

28¾"

19"

3½"

DOUBLE DRESSER

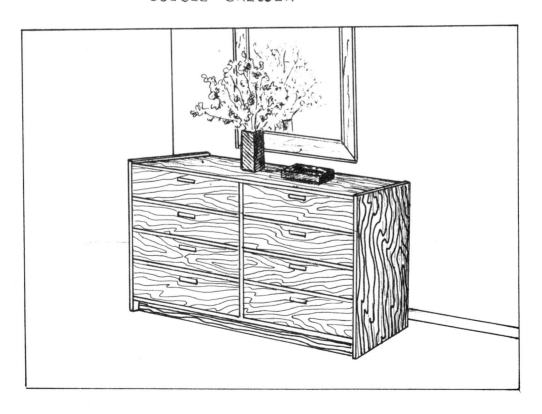

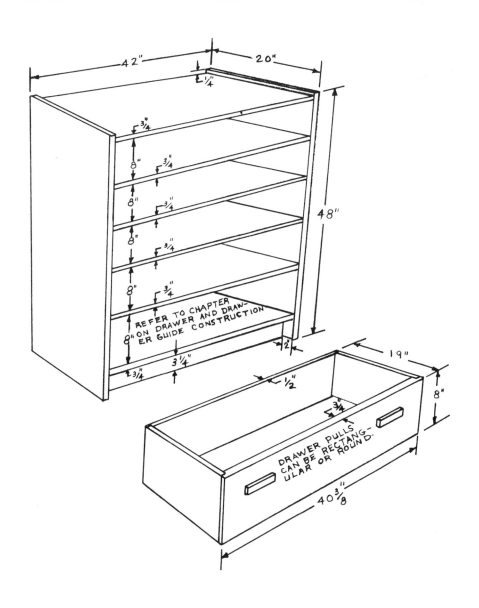

42" 20"
¼"
¾"
8" ¾"
8" ¾"
8" ¾"
8" ¾"
48"
REFER TO CHAPTER
ON DRAWER AND DRAW-
ER GUIDE CONSTRUCTION
8"
2"
3¼"
¾"

19"
½"
¾"
8"
DRAWER PULLS
CAN BE RECTANG-
ULAR OR ROUND.
40⅜"

CHEST OF FIVE DRAWERS

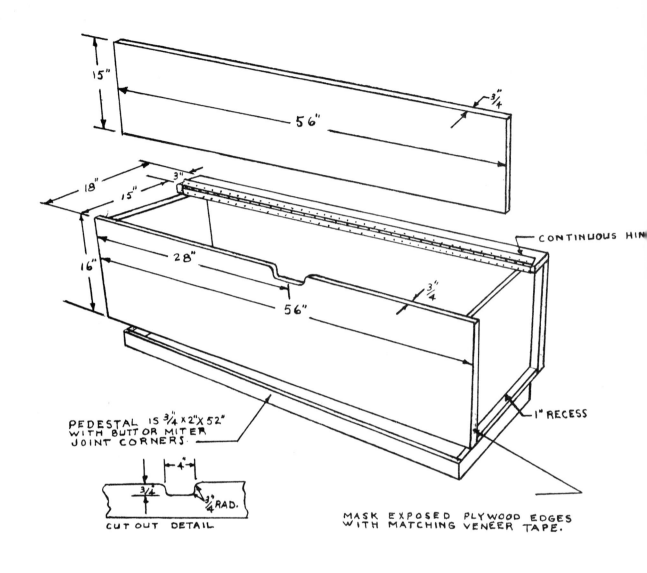

15"

56"

3/4"

18"

3"

15"

CONTINUOUS HIN

16"

28"

56"

3/4"

3/4"

1" RECESS

PEDESTAL IS 3/4"x2"x52"
WITH BUTT OR MITER
JOINT CORNERS.

4"

3/4"

3/4" RAD.

CUT OUT DETAIL

MASK EXPOSED PLYWOOD EDGES
WITH MATCHING VENEER TAPE.

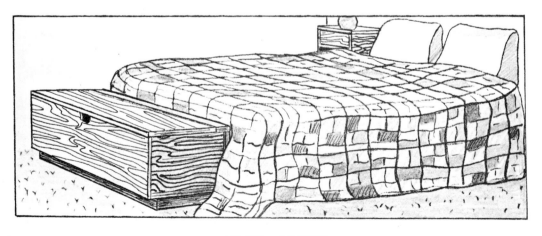

HOPE CHEST

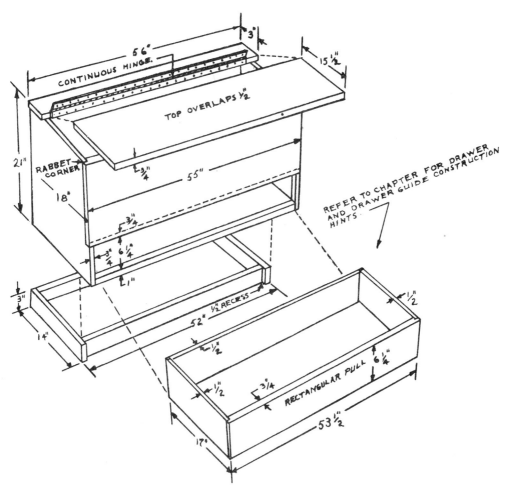

CONTINUOUS HINGE.

56"

3"

15 1/2"

TOP OVERLAPS 1/2"

21"

RABBET CORNER

3/4"

18"

55"

REFER TO CHAPTER FOR DRAWER AND DRAWER GUIDE CONSTRUCTION HINTS.

3/4"

3" 6 1/4"
4

1"

3"

1/2 RECESS

52"

1/2"

14"

1/2"

1"
2

3/4

RECTANGULAR PULL

6 1/4"

17"

53 1/2"

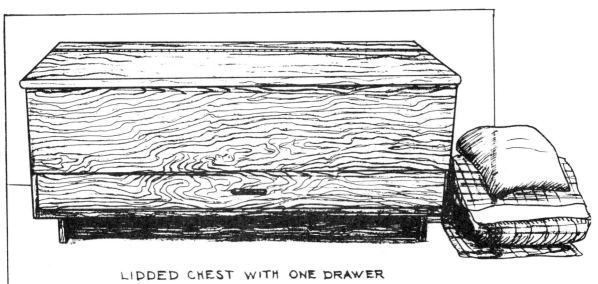

LIDDED CHEST WITH ONE DRAWER

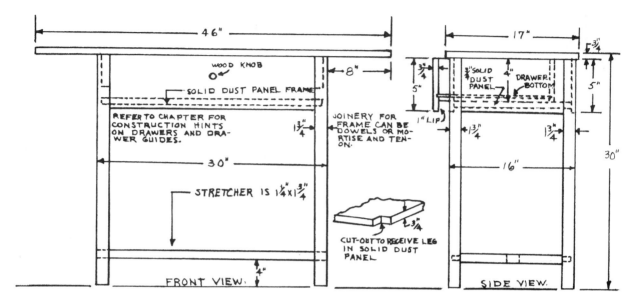

46"

WOOD KNOB

SOLID DUST PANEL FRAME

REFER TO CHAPTER FOR
CONSTRUCTION HINTS
ON DRAWERS AND DRA-
WER GUIDES.

STRETCHER IS 1¼"X1¾"

8"

JOINERY FOR
FRAME CAN BE
DOWELS OR MO-
RTISE AND TEN-
ON.

1¾"

30"

CUT-OUT TO RECEIVE LEG
IN SOLID DUST
PANEL

4"

FRONT VIEW.

17"

¾"

¾"

5"

¾" SOLID
DUST
PANEL

4"

DRAWER
BOTTOM

¾"

5"

1" LIP

1¾"

1¾"

16"

30"

SIDE VIEW.

DRESSING TABLE

DRESSING TABLE, STOOL AND MIRROR
STOOL AND MIRROR PLANS ARE ON FOLLOWING PAGE.

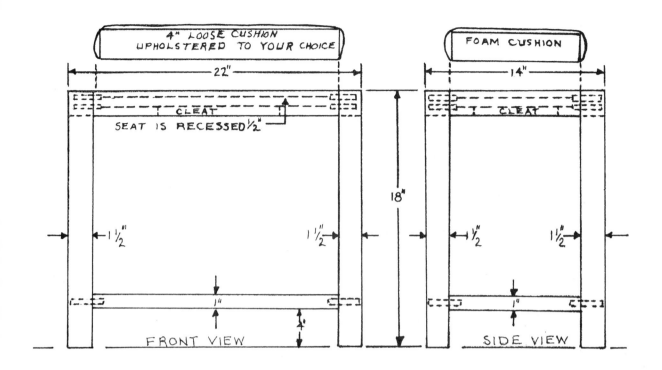

4" LOOSE CUSHION
UPHOLSTERED TO YOUR CHOICE

FOAM CUSHION

22"

14"

18"

CLEAT

SEAT IS RECESSED ½"

CLEAT

1½"

1½"

½"

1½"

1"

1"

4"

FRONT VIEW

SIDE VIEW

MATCHING STOOL TO DRESSING TABLE.

MATCHING MIRROR

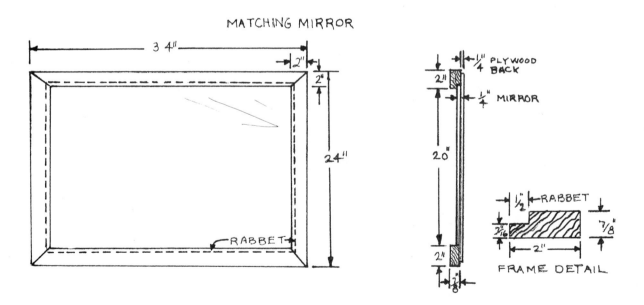

3'4"

2"

2"

24"

RABBET

¼" PLYWOOD BACK

2"

¼" MIRROR

20"

2"

1½" RABBET

2/16"

7/8"

2"

FRAME DETAIL

2/8"

DOUBLE BED

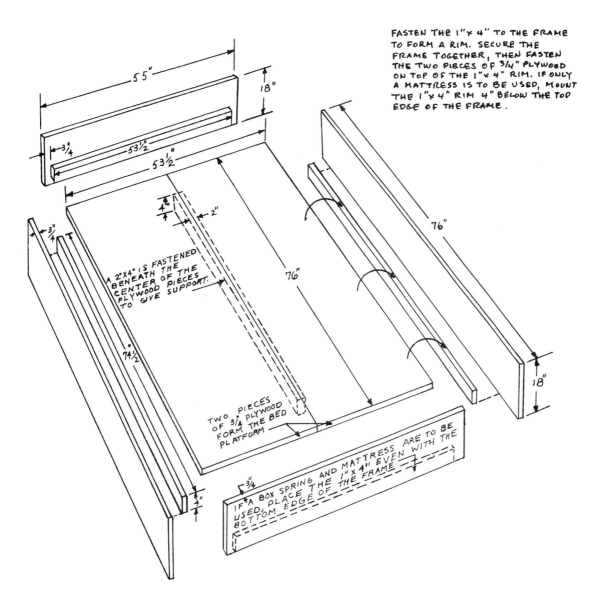

FASTEN THE 1"x 4" TO THE FRAME TO FORM A RIM. SECURE THE FRAME TOGETHER, THEN FASTEN THE TWO PIECES OF 3/4" PLYWOOD ON TOP OF THE 1"x 4" RIM. IF ONLY A MATTRESS IS TO BE USED, MOUNT THE 1"x 4" RIM 4" BELOW THE TOP EDGE OF THE FRAME.

55"

18"

3/4"

53 1/2"

53 1/2"

4"

2"

76"

A 2"x4" IS FASTENED BENEATH THE CENTER OF THE PLYWOOD PIECES TO GIVE SUPPORT.

76"

18"

74 1/2"

TWO PIECES OF 3/4 PLYWOOD FORM THE BED PLATFORM

3/4"

4"

3/4"

IF A BOX SPRING AND MATTRESS ARE TO BE USED, PLACE THE 1"x 4" EVEN WITH THE BOTTOM EDGE OF THE FRAME.

CORNERS CAN BE A SIMPLE BUTT OR RABBET JOINT.

BUNK BEDS

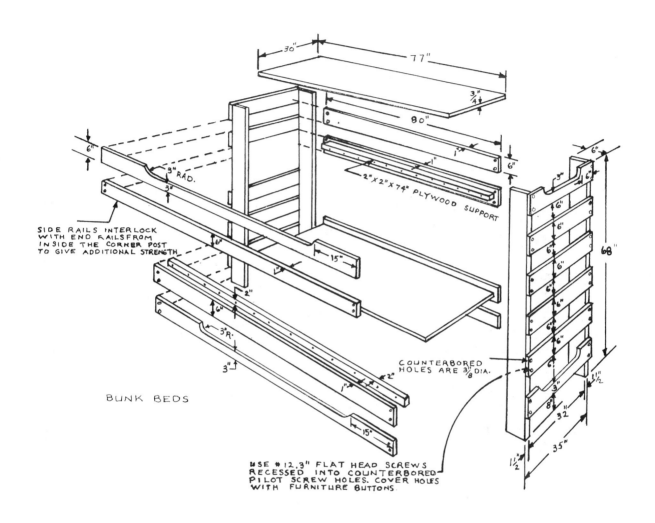

30"

77"

3/4"

80"

6"

6"

6"

2"X2"X74" PLYWOOD SUPPORT

1"

1"

3" RAD.

3"

3"

4"

6"

6"

SIDE RAILS INTERLOCK
WITH END RAILS FROM
INSIDE THE CORNER POST
TO GIVE ADDITIONAL STRENGTH

6"

6"

6"

6"

6"

6"

68"

15"

1"

2"

6"

COUNTERBORED
HOLES ARE 3/8" DIA.

3"

1½"

3" R.

8"

32"

3"

1½"

35"

2"

1"

BUNK BEDS

15"

1½"

USE #12, 3" FLAT HEAD SCREWS
RECESSED INTO COUNTERBORED
PILOT SCREW HOLES. COVER HOLES
WITH FURNITURE BUTTONS.

DOUBLE BED

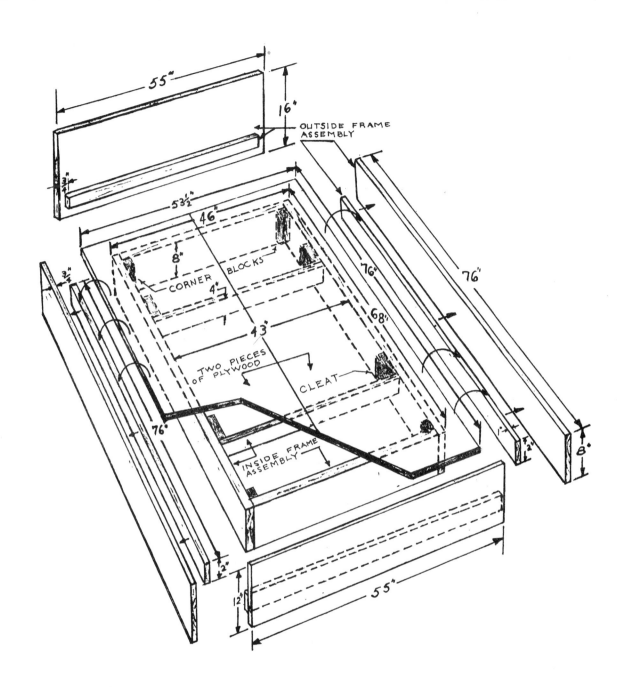

55"

16"

OUTSIDE FRAME
ASSEMBLY

3"

53½"

46"

8"

CORNER BLOCKS

4"

7

43"

TWO PIECES
OF PLYWOOD

CLEAT

68"

76"

76"

76"

3¼"

76"

INSIDE FRAME
ASSEMBLY

2"

1"

2"

8"

2"

12"

55"

WHEN 1"x2"s ARE FASTENED TO
OUTSIDE FRAME, SCREW THE
PLYWOOD TO THE TOP EDGE
OF THE 1"x2" BOARDS. WHEN
PLYWOOD IS SECURED, LIFT
THE OUTSIDE FRAME ASSEM-
BLY TO PLACE OVER THE
INSIDE FRAME ASSEMBLY.

WALL-MOUNTED HEADBOARD AND NIGHT TABLES.
THE BED PLANS ARE ON THE NEXT PAGE.

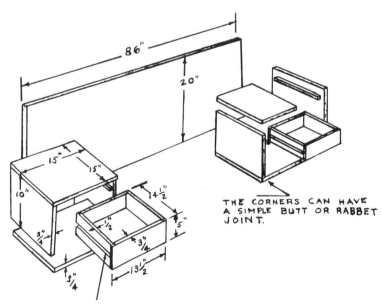

86"

20"

15"

15"

10"

3"/4

4 1/2"

5"

1/2"

3"/4

3"/4

13 1/2"

THE CORNERS CAN HAVE
A SIMPLE BUTT OR RABBET
JOINT.

METAL OR WOOD DRAWER GUIDES.
REFER TO CHAP. IN THIS BOOK.

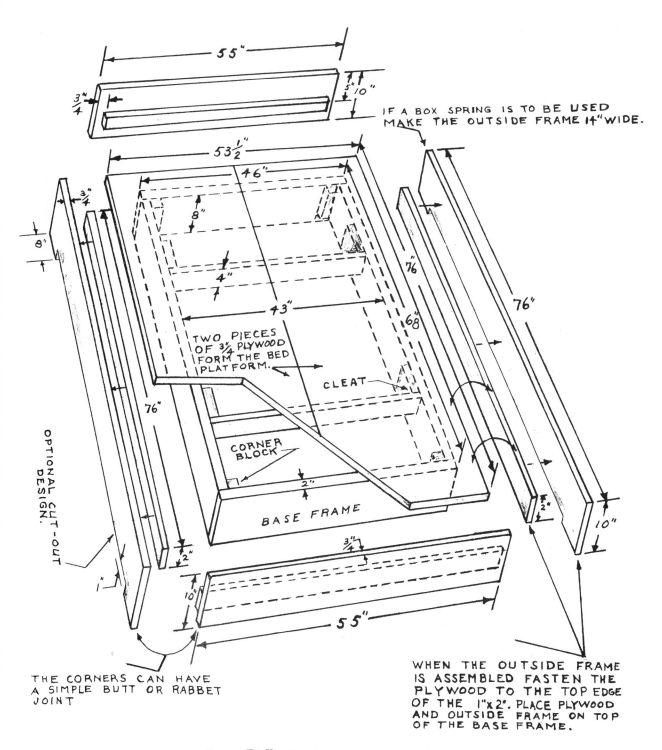

55"

3/4"

5" 10"

IF A BOX SPRING IS TO BE USED
MAKE THE OUTSIDE FRAME 14" WIDE.

53 1/2"

46"

3/4"

8'

8"

4"

76"

76"

43"

68"

76"

TWO PIECES
OF 3/4 PLYWOOD
FORM THE BED
PLATFORM.

CLEAT

76"

CORNER
BLOCK

2"

BASE FRAME

2"

2"

10"

OPTIONAL CUT-OUT
DESIGN.

2"

1"

3/4"

10"

55"

THE CORNERS CAN HAVE
A SIMPLE BUTT OR RABBET
JOINT

WHEN THE OUTSIDE FRAME
IS ASSEMBLED FASTEN THE
PLYWOOD TO THE TOP EDGE
OF THE 1"x 2". PLACE PLYWOOD
AND OUTSIDE FRAME ON TOP
OF THE BASE FRAME.

DOUBLE BED

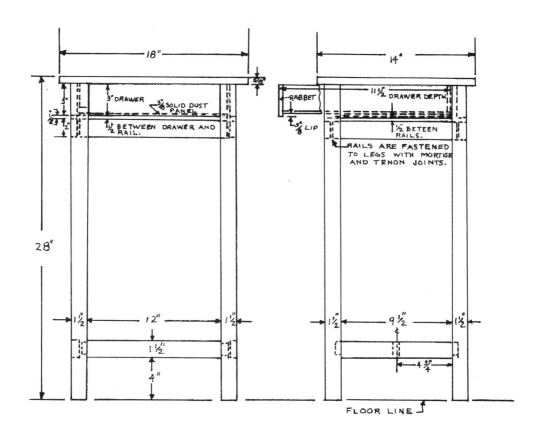

18"

⅝"

3" DRAWER
⅜ SOLID DUST PANEL

1½" BETWEEN DRAWER AND RAIL.

28"

1½"   12"   1½"

1½"

4"

14"

RABBET

11½ DRAWER DEPTH

⅝" LIP

½ BETEEN RAILS.

RAILS ARE FASTENED TO LEGS WITH MORTISE AND TENON JOINTS.

1½"   9½"   1½"

4¾"

FLOOR LINE

SMALL TABLE

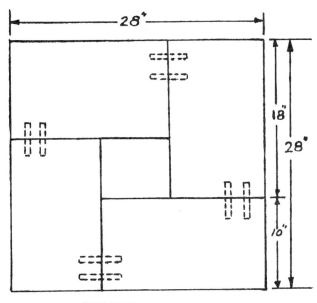

STEP I
DOWEL AND GLUE THE
FOUR BOARDS WITH
EACH JOINT STAGGERED.

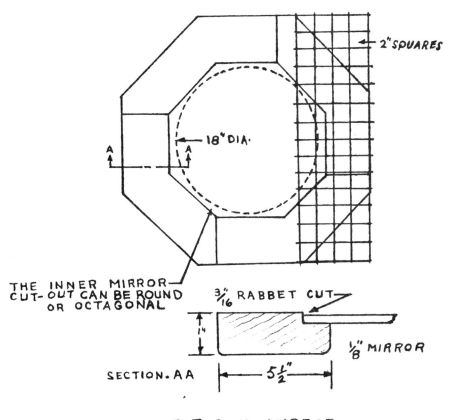

2" SQUARES

18" DIA.

A

THE INNER MIRROR
CUT-OUT CAN BE ROUND
OR OCTAGONAL

3/16" RABBET CUT

1/8" MIRROR

SECTION. AA

5 1/2"

OCTAGON MIRROR

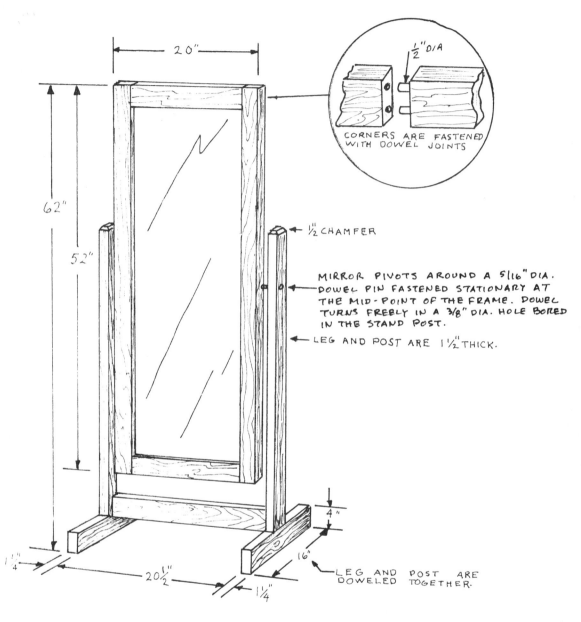

20"

62"

52"

$\frac{1}{2}$" DIA

CORNERS ARE FASTENED
WITH DOWEL JOINTS

$\frac{1}{2}$" CHAMFER

MIRROR PIVOTS AROUND A $\frac{5}{16}$" DIA.
DOWEL PIN FASTENED STATIONARY AT
THE MID-POINT OF THE FRAME. DOWEL
TURNS FREELY IN A $\frac{3}{8}$" DIA. HOLE BORED
IN THE STAND POST.

LEG AND POST ARE $1\frac{1}{2}$" THICK.

4"

$1\frac{1}{4}$"

$20\frac{1}{2}$"

$1\frac{1}{4}$"

16"

LEG AND POST ARE
DOWELED TOGETHER.

FULL LENGTH DRESSING MIRROR

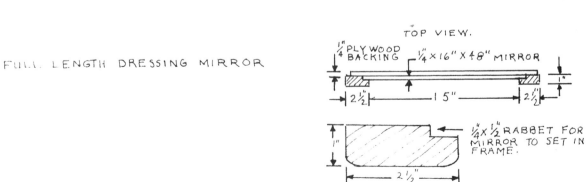

TOP VIEW.

$\frac{1}{4}$" PLYWOOD
BACKING

$\frac{1}{4}$" X 16" X 48" MIRROR

$2\frac{1}{2}$"

15"

$2\frac{1}{2}$"

1"

$\frac{1}{4}$" X $\frac{1}{2}$" RABBET FOR
MIRROR TO SET IN
FRAME.

1"

$2\frac{1}{2}$"

Index